Age of
Minority

Age of Minority

3 solo plays by

Jordan Tannahill

Playwrights Canada Press
Toronto

LIBRARY AND ARCHIVES CANADA CATALOGUING IN PUBLICATION
Tannahill, Jordan
[Plays. Selections]
        Age of minority : three solo plays / Jordan Tannahill.

Get yourself home Skyler James -- Peter Fechter : 59 minutes -- rihannaboi95.

Issued in print and electronic formats.
ISBN 978-1-77091-194-9 (pbk.).-- ISBN 978-1-77091-195-6 (pdf).--
ISBN 978-1-77091-196-3 (epub)

        1. Gays--Drama. I. Title.

PS8639.A579A6 2013   C812'.6   C2013-904418-3
                                                 C2013-904419-1

We acknowledge the financial support of the Canada Council for the Arts, the Ontario Arts Council (OAC)—an agency of the Government of Ontario, which last year funded 1,681 individual artists and 1,125 organizations in 216 communities across Ontario for a total of $52.8 million—the Ontario Media Development Corporation, and the Government of Canada through the Canada Book Fund for our publishing activities.

I wish to dedicate this book to my parents, Karen and Bruce, who taught me the importance of speaking up for those who have been silenced.

Preface

This collection presents three young people backed up against walls, metaphorically and literally, who risk everything for a chance to love and to be loved. And all three, to some extent, are queer. Beyond a merely sexual understanding of the word, they refuse the norms they are confronted with. They are sublime outcasts. Written between the ages of nineteen and twenty-four, the three plays also give voice to my own coming of age.

Get Yourself Home Skyler James was written after I befriended the real-life Skyler James in the summer of 2008 and, over a series of conversations that year, she related her story to me. By the time I sat down to write the play, I knew her voice and journey so intimately that I was able to write her monologue from beginning to end in a single sitting. While I have attempted to be as true to Skyler's story as possible, I have taken certain fictional liberties for the sake of dramatic action and clarity.

rihannaboi95 arose out of time I spent facilitating drama workshops at youth shelters in Toronto with the theatre company Project:

Humanity. I left wanting to tell the story of a queer youth who is forced from his/her home. The form of the piece revealed itself a year later when my friend Jon Davies introduced me to the proliferation of YouTube videos being made by preteen and teenage boys dancing and lip-synching to pop songs by female divas. These videos were such uncensored and unself-conscious expressions of their inner selves. I was compelled to know who these youth were, what prompted them to record these videos, to put them online, and what the fallout might be from doing so. It also unlocked a lot of exciting theatrical opportunities for us.

Traditionally the monologue in Western theatre has had four primary directives: an address to God, an address to the audience, an address to another character, and an address to the self. With the advent of YouTube there is a fifth. On a daily basis people confess their inner-most thoughts to an anonymous online viewership in a manner that functions somewhat as a combination of the pre-existing four directives. YouTube listens much like God does: silent, absent, and omnipotent. But then YouTube videos are made to be viewed by people, and thus an address to YouTube is an address to an audience. Or perhaps we make a video that addresses a specific individual, like a fan video to a celebrity. But more often than not we are alone when we address YouTube, and alone when we watch YouTube. We often find a way to be more vulnerable and candid with YouTube than in any other capacity of our lives, which is why YouTube, perhaps above all else, is the ultimate conversation with one's self.

Finally, *Peter Fechter: 59 Minutes* is a play inspired by a photograph: the image of an eighteen-year-old boy being pulled from the Berlin Wall's Death Strip—an image I first saw when I myself was eighteen. I spent five years—from my adolescence into early adulthood—inserting myself into that photograph, trying to understand how someone could be driven to take such a risk. While I have tried to capture many aspects of Peter's real life, in the end my research could only bring me so far. The burning questions I had about Peter—what was going through his head in the moments before he jumped, in the moments after he was shot—could not be found in the official records but rather in my own heart and imagination. As such, I see this play as half a portrait of the real Peter and half a portrait of my own coming of age. Ultimately I hope it is both a document of a specific event and a universal meditation on what we sacrifice for love and all that we risk to gain and lose as we enter the world of adults.

Having spent much of my own youth with these three individuals, I feel very blessed to now have the opportunity to share them with you.

—Jordan Tannahill

Get Yourself Home
Skyler James

On Being Skyler
by Natasha Greenblatt

Get Yourself Home Skyler James wasn't your typical TYA touring
experience where you might set up and perform in a different school
auditorium every day. My stage manager and I stayed in each school
for a week, touring individual classrooms, carrying one flat and three
milk crates up and down stairs, and running the show two to four
times every day. It was the most terrifyingly intimate acting experience I have ever had, at times only inches away from a front row of
desks and teenage faces.

One of my best experiences was in a portable at R.H. King
Academy in Scarborough. We'd set up the night before in the wrong
portable. The group of students we were supposed to perform for
was tiny and the teacher from the mistaken portable took us aside
and asked if we wanted to leave our set where it was, bring the orig-
inal class there, and perform for a larger audience. It was a magical
show. The room was filled to the brim with students, all excited by
the break from their daily routine. They listened, laughed, and asked
fascinating questions during the talkback after the show.

Performing Skyler challenged my assumptions about Toronto. Earl Haig, a school known for its intensive arts program, and a school I thought would be one of the more progressive environments, was the place I felt the most intolerance (albeit from a teacher). Northern Secondary had elected a transgendered school president the year before and had an active Gay–Straight Alliance, but I experienced an almost complacent sense of self-satisfaction. It was there someone said homophobia was "not a problem anymore," although when I asked some of the GSA members I was told the word "gay" was still commonly used as an insult.

At R.H. King I'd been warned the large Tamil population might have difficulty with the homosexual content. But the students there were some of the most receptive, engaging in honest and in-depth discussions. One young woman spoke about the challenges of coming from an immigrant family where the attitude towards homosexuality at home was different than the mainstream attitude she was increasingly identifying with in her chosen community.

"I think the 'Don't Ask Don't Tell Policy' is good," said one young man from Central Tech, "I wouldn't want to know if my best friend was gay because then I'd feel weird hanging out with him." A young black man responded, "It shouldn't matter if you're gay, just like it shouldn't matter what race you are."

Performing a Texan lesbian war resister/deserter seeking refugee status for grade eleven students at nine in the morning may be one of the most challenging acting experiences I will ever have. I had to learn how to keep their attention despite fire drills, announcements over the PA, and some overzealous sign-language interpreters. But it will also live in my memory as one of the most fulfilling.

I bumped into one student on the subway a few days after I'd performed for her class. We spoke about the effect the show had on her and her fellow students. "Oh, and one other thing," she said as the subway doors opened, "we all want to know. Are you gay, in real life?" "Does it matter?" I asked as the doors closed. "No, no it doesn't," she said.

Get Yourself Home Skyler James was first produced by Roseneath Theatre as a touring classroom play in the fall of 2009, with the following cast and crew:

Directed by Alisa Palmer
Performed by Natasha Greenblatt
Set design by Lucinda Zak
Stage management by Krista MacIsaac

The production travelled to five high schools within the Toronto District School Board (TDSB). It took up residency at each school for a week and was performed for one class at a time, sometimes up to four times a day. The play was selected as a flagship project for the TDSB's newly introduced Equity Curriculum, which, for the first time in Canada, made efforts to include sexual orientation and gender identity in high-school curricula. Natasha Greenblatt received a 2010 Dora Mavor Moore Award for her performance as Skyler James.

SKYLER James, a young woman of twenty, busies herself unpacking boxes of frozen chicken and placing the frozen nuggets on baking trays in the basement of an Ottawa KFC. She talks to Rebecca, her girlfriend and co-worker, who has locked herself in the employee washroom.

SKYLER eventually sits on a box of thawing frozen chicken.

SKYLER
Well it ain't like I killed someone, Becca! How am I supposed to explain myself if you won't even open the door?

Pause.

Listen, I know you're probably thinking a hundred and one things right now... those police officers showing up this morning... but I bet none of 'em are even half true.

Pause.

Come on, Becca, I got a buttload of frozen chicken out here and if you don't come out and help we're gonna have a soggy mess! Becca?

Long pause.

Wanna know something crazy? I used to think Colonel Sanders was my grampa. My grandma told me he was once. Kids believe that stuff. There used to be one down the street and I'd go there sometimes and I'd talk to him. Talk to the friggin' Colonel like he was my grampa and I'd tell him all sorts of things. Later found out my real one was like hit by a freight train after getting shit-faced one night. So my grandma had a good reason to make up that story. She lived in this old house, way too big for her. Every day after school I'd go and try to live there. Try to convince her to take me in. And we'd like watch cartoons for a couple hours and eat sandwiches, but when it got dark she'd always say: "All right, time to get yourself home, Skyler James." And I'd walk back up Power Plant Road, past the KFC, and the Colonel would be there glowing and I'd stop and I'd pray to him. To convince Grandma to take me in. Every night. Isn't that crazy? And when I figured out I was a dyke, you know who I was most worried about finding out? The Colonel!

Listen, I know there's a lot of stuff I ain't told you about. I mean stuff I really, really should've told you, but I was scared, you know? Like maybe you'd think I was some sort of… I don't know, like criminal or something. Budgie? Jesus, Becca, you want Amir to come down and bust this door down? His break'll be over any minute now.

Pause.

All right. You wanna know the kinda trouble I've been in? "My deal" as you call it; you wanna know "my deal"? First of all everything I told you about being in the Army and being from Texas and all that stuff, I mean that's all true, I never lied to you...

You wanna know where it all started?

Beat.

I was fingered in the local Target.

Laughs.

You have to understand there was only one dyke in Wichita Falls: her name was Lisa and she had a buzz cut and one EXCO sweatsuit she wore every friggin' day, no word of a lie. Well like I was just shopping by myself just trying on stuff? Just like jeans and stuff and she was looking at all the underwear they got there. And we sorta nodded at each other; I was always friendly to her and whatever. Not like most people. So we started like talking and it was pretty easy. Wasn't nearly as pretty as you are. Well we must've been talking for damn near forty minutes before she said, "Guess you better try on those jeans." So we walked over to the change rooms and she said she'd wait for me. And like... I don't know what it was but all of a sudden I was like, "You wanna help?" I didn't even know what that meant... Maybe like a second opinion or whatever. But she didn't ask or nothing. She just walked into the stall with me and that was that. I was a lesbian. Lisa lived in like this Winnebago? With her mom. Her mom was Indian of some sort. We both loved N.E.R.D and Ludacris and Timbaland; oh man, when Soulja Boy came out we thought it was psycho good. She taught me the whole dance and everything. One time we did the dance right in the middle of a Walmart!

Anyway, couple weeks later we were walking through the mall? I'd gone and cut my hair short. I'd started wearing baseball caps. I mean I don't even know the first thing about baseball! It didn't make no sense. We were on our way to Dairy Queen when we walked by this recruitin' station. It was right between the Dairy Queen and Walmart. So you could buy some jeans, join the Army, and get some ice cream. And this place had all those big posters and cardboard cut-outs of helicopters and videos of soldiers saving people from floods and stuff; I mean they had the whole nine yards. So we walked in, sorta for like a joke, I guess. We were bored. Frig all to do in Wichita Falls on a Sunday unless you're into God and stuff, which is bigger than baseball where I come from. And the recruiter guy behind the counter, he started pulling like this salesman pitch on us, telling us we're gonna see the world and that they were gonna pay for our college and that if we joined right then they'd even give us this big sign-on bonus. And I was about to say we weren't really interested or nothing when I looked over and Lisa was already filling out the paperwork. And then, without really thinking about it, I started filling it out too. When it was all done the guy gave us this big, shiny information-package thing and we walked out. You know you'd think we'd start talking about it, trying to figure out what it'd all be like. But we didn't. We just walked next door and bought Blizzards and that was that. They were really good…

Beat.

You remember the first time I saw you? I was coming in here for my interview and you came out from round back, and you'd been cleaning the deep fryer so you were just like totally covered in grease. I remember thinking you were the most beautiful girl in the whole world, even more than that Milla Jovovitch. But I'm more of a brains girl, you know? Like how you can do all those crosswords or like… like when Lisa fixed up that white pickup of mine with a wrench and some elbow grease, now I mean *that's* a woman. We drove that piece of scrap metal up four states to Kentucky.

You know Fort Campbell wasn't much different than high school. 'Lotta concrete, gym class, a caf. I signed up to be a mechanic, don't ask me why. Not like I even knew that much about cars; I mean I'd only been a dyke for about a month. So when I got to Fort Campbell I worked in the motor pool. Working mostly with Jeeps and LAVs… you know like light-armoured vehicles or whatever. Carburetors, fuel injectors, just changing the tires, you know, I've done it all. I was good too. I have small hands. Which is good. Lots of guys in the motor pool would talk 'bout Iraq. Lots of ghost stories. Land mines; little kids with grenades. Some of 'em would joke around about crap they'd done over there? Real bad stuff too, like giving people beatings and stuff. One of the grease monkeys, Private Sheen? he'd stepped on an IED and had these big scars all across his face. So um… I mean I don't really know what more to say about that… it was pretty boring I guess. Lisa got posted on the other side of the base but we still saw each other in the Kfec. That's the caf. The Army's got names for everything. We'd eat together. Oh man they had these crazy good spicy fries! It's all we'd eat.

Listen, I know what you're thinking. That we were lezing it up; that we were asking for it. Everyone thinks that but it ain't true. I swear to you we weren't lezing it up. We made a decision. First or second night we got there. That we'd like never hold hands or talk romantic or nothing. So we never did anything, welllllll… okay that's not totally true. One night she came over just to like… hang out in my room or whatever. Play some *Guitar Hero*. And we started making out. And like… well we took some pictures and stuff. I mean how else was I gonna last? It wasn't a lot, just like eight or nine. Just so I could remember. When she wasn't around. But other than that we were just two normal girls, right? Just two normal girls who ate their spicy fries together in the Kfec; that was it, end of story.

SKYLER *returns to placing nuggets on the trays.*

C'mon, Budgie, I got like a million boxes left! I can't do it all on my own!

Beat. She mutters.

'Sides, I feel like an idiot talking to this door.

Pause.

You know, you can hide all you want but I couldn't. They were living right across the hall from me. Used to call them the Bud Boys. They were always drinking Bud in their rooms. They'd get it from the gas station, twenty bucks for a pack of thirty. "Cheaper than pop." The Bud Boys were from Nashville. Their rooms were all covered in these photographs from this like one friggin' time they went to Coyote Ugly together during recruitment week. That's the week they send us all back to our hometowns to recruit our friends to join the Army. Most guys just blow their signing bonus on booze. One of them kept playing this Kid Rock CD for like three weeks straight; I'm not even joking, must've played it six times a day, seven days a week. So I always kept my door shut. They started calling me Hermit the Crab. And then just Crabs. "Hey Crabs, what's scratching?" They'd say that all the time. They loved that one.

One night I was coming back from the motor pool and I was real tired and sore and I got to my room and the door's open. Just wide open. And I walked in and there they were: the friggin' Bud Boys huddled around my laptop. "Hey Crabs"—but before they could say anything I shouted "Get outta here, get the frig outta here!" "Hey Crabs, nice tits. Which ones are yours?!" And then I realized what they were looking at and I felt like I was gonna puke, like I was gonna spill all my guts right there, and they were laughing and spitting like a bunch of dogs, like friggin' dogs do when they're chewing through trash. "GET OUT!" And I went nuts. Like I started hitting them with my fists and they were howling like a bunch of dogs. "GET OUT, GET OUT!" And I slammed the door and I could hear them in the hall blabbing to all the other Bud Boys, and somewhere someone was playing friggin' Kid Rock's "Sweet Home Alabama." And I went over to my laptop and there was Lisa and me on my bed. I started looking through the pictures… I noticed her face wasn't in any of 'em. I just remember how relieved I felt 'bout that.

I didn't sleep that night. Didn't leave my room. Played lots of *Guitar Hero*. You think I play a lot now? You have no idea; got so I could play almost any song perfect, no joke. Next morning I went straight to the motor pool, didn't wanna eat nothing, didn't want to see no one in the Kfec. 'Specially not Lisa. I was changing tires when the guys came in. They were just messing around by the loading bay and I heard Private Sheen saying something about carpet munching. I just kept my eyes to the tires. They started working, no one saying nothing. They were doing something on the exhaust. I was thinking good, no big deal. And then all of a sudden I was in the air. I looked down and Private Sheen was holding me, right above his head, and all the guys were laughing, and he started like shaking me and saying, "Look, boys, I caught me a dyke. I caught me my very own dyke!" And I started kickin' and he dropped me. Dropped me right on my back on the friggin' concrete. I couldn't breathe. I just lay there gaping like a fish and they were laughing. Then the sergeant piped up. Started shouting for everyone to get back to work; told me to get up off the ground, didn't even ask why I was limping, didn't even ask why they were all laughing. You know what I think? I think he was there the whole time. He knew. And either he knew and didn't care, or he knew and was in on it.

At lunch I saw Lisa in the Kfec. I sat down beside her and I told her; I said, "We can't do this anymore." "What you talking about?" she said. "I mean we can't sit beside one another, we can't talk to one another, we can't do nothing together anymore, you hear?" I told her 'bout the Bud Boys and the laptop. "But don't worry, none of the pics have your face in 'em." But I knew if we kept hanging around together they'd start going after her too. So I picked up my tray and walked away. It wasn't like I started crying or nothing. We didn't have one of those Hollywood romances. We were just trying to survive.

Pause.

Nothing like you and me have.

I got back from the Kfec and found like a sticky note on my door? When I got inside I like read it. It said "Fort Campbell's got no room for dykes like you." I started taking meals in my room after that. And every night I got back from the motor pool there'd be another note on my door. Lisa and I talked over MSN almost every night. But I still didn't tell her. Like I told her everything but I didn't tell her about them notes. I guess I was afraid she'd say something like, "Oh they're just joking" or "They're just dirty words." But there were ideas tied to them words. Real, ugly ideas.

When I wasn't playing *Guitar Hero*, I'd spend a lot of time by myself on the Internet? And one night I come across this website some guy had made for his buddy. This buddy of his was named Barry Winchell; he'd been a private at Fort Campbell four years before I got there and had already seen two tours of duty over in Afghaniland. Well when it was found out he was gay, another private named Calvin Glover beat him to death with a baseball bat. Right in his bed. You can google him yourself. Private Barry Winchell. The Army did a probe? And the report came back saying there wasn't any "climate of homophobia" on the base. And then a month later, Fort Campbell's very own General Robert Clark was promoted to lieutenant general. And you know the crazy thing about it? Both boys were in my unit. One hundred and first Airborne Division. Whole thing happened eight doors down! I walked by the room every morning and every night from the motor pool! One of the Bud Boys lived in it now. Had a big Nickelback poster hanging on the wall.

So I emailed this guy who made like this website for Barry Winchell or whatever? I think he lived in Topeka. I told him who I was and where I was and all about the sticky notes. He emailed me right back, like an hour later, with all this information on like war deserters. I didn't know what to think about it. It scared me so much I closed the email. Like I was watching porn or something. I felt ashamed even looking at it.

The notes kept coming. For two whole months. Whenever I'd see Lisa in the halls we'd like smile or whatever, but soon she was sitting with other girls in the Kfec. She started liking it more, you know? The drills, the food, the outings. Started going to more functions and stuff. So we began talking less over MSN. Then once a whole week went by and we didn't talk at all. After I beat all the songs on *Guitar Hero* I got real into this zombie game. I ever show you that one? Where you wake up in this shopping mall and you're all alone. And you got like this gun, right? And basically you just go round shooting all the zombies and picking up ammo and grenades... But oh man if you blew a zombie's arm off they'd pick it up and start beating you with it! Can you believe that? They'd start beating you with their own friggin' arms; oh man it was so funny. And whenever I'd get bored of running around the shopping mall I'd open up that email. The one about the war deserters? And all the people helping them across the States? It felt like they were, I don't know, like wizards, and everyone else in the world were muggles. Like only other wizards knew they existed, you know what I'm talking about, right?

SKYLER gets up, crosses to the bathroom door, and slides to the ground with her back against it.

I can hear you breathing.

Beat.

Do you want me to stop? Just say it and I'll stop. Tell me to go away and I will, I'll walk right outta this basement.

Long pause.

I'm tired, Budgie. I don't want to do this no more.

Long pause.

You ever been so tired you thought you were a ghost?

We were doing training exercises behind the base. In this big field.
Weren't allowed to sleep for four days straight. They kept us running
through mud. Sitting. Watching. Waiting. Until we lost our minds.
They'd light flares and we'd have to run to them. Drills all night.
Snake in the Grass. Never been so cold in my life. There were like
knives in my lungs. I found myself leaning up against this big boul-
der. I hadn't heard anyone shout for hours. Maybe they forgot about
me. I was sitting there when I swore the sky got a shade brighter. So
little I bet no one in the world noticed but me. And then it started
snowing. It started snowing! At first I thought I was imagining it
but I wasn't; I mean I could feel it on my face. I'd never seen snow
before. Like I'd seen like pictures and stuff but never the real thing.

Beat.

I never felt so far from home in my life.

SKYLER *stands and walks slowly back over to her box of melting
chicken.*

When I got back there was another note on my door. I just ripped
it down, went into my room. I was too tired to sleep so I played my
game for a few hours before I got a headache. And I was in the middle
of changing when I reached into my pocket and found the note. I

took it out and I read it. And that's when I knew I had to get out. You wanna know what it said? "We're gonna give you a dicking tonight to turn you straight." And then right below: "PS We stole the keys to your room from Sarge's office."

I was so tired from them four days in the field, don't know how I was thinking straight. I sent a text to Lisa. "Take care of yourself." And I just started like grabbing crap and stuffing it into bags. Clothes, CDs, my TV: I stuffed my whole TV into this duffle bag. I didn't know what to take or what to leave: my clock radio, my photographs, my blanket, my shoes… I was just like cramming in as much as I could. I felt like I was missing stuff; missing bags, missing clothes. And I was making for the door when I heard a knock. I froze. "Who is it?" I heard Lisa's voice. "It's me." I grabbed the door, pulled her in, and shut it. She looked around the room and before she could even say something I started telling her about the notes and about how they were planning on coming that night and raping me, and I'd never said the word out loud like that before, but there it was and it just thudded on the ground like a big pile of dirty laundry. "You think they're gonna rape you?" I could tell she didn't believe me but it didn't matter. My mind was made up. She asked me where I thought I was going and I said, "Canada, I guess." Well my Spanish wasn't so hot so I really didn't have any other options. I asked her to help me carry my bags to the pickup. She thought about that one for a real long time, so long I thought maybe she didn't hear me ask. But then she grabbed the duffle bag. "Jesus, you got a TV in here?" I told her if anyone asked we were just getting it fixed, which was crazy 'cause it was damn near past midnight.

We snuck into the hall, tried our best to avoid them CCT cameras, and bolted for the back doors. Nearly ripped the bags open dragging them across the parking lot. It was cold out. Felt like a rain was coming on. I chucked everything into the back of the pickup. Lisa asked me if I was going to be driving past the twenty-four-hour Walmart and I said I would be. So we drove out and the whole time she was trying to tell me this was a bad idea and that I should just tell my sarge and all this stuff. I just drove, not saying nothing. When we got to the Walmart it was drizzling so I went in with Lisa and bought a tarp to cover up all my stuff in the back. I don't think she even bought anything. Maybe she just wanted to spend a little more time together. 'Cause like I think we both knew this was gonna be the last time. In the parking lot we threw the tarp over the back and she helped me tie it down. And then it really started to rain. I asked her how she was getting back and she said she'd wait for the shuttle. I kissed her. Real gentle right on her nose. And then she started crying for real. I told her to promise not to tell anyone and she promised.

I pulled onto the highway around like two in the morning and I slipped in some Biggie.

She starts reciting "Long Kiss Goodnight" by the Notorious B.I.G.

Oh man, Budgie, back then I knew all the words. I kept telling myself I was going on a holiday. Like maybe to Disneyland. I love Disneyland. I never been to Disneyland but I love it. I was shouting along with Biggie to keep myself awake. Well I hadn't slept for four days, what would you do? I was driving and I'd start looking at like the white lines on the road flashing by: whoosh, whoosh, whoosh. A car's headlights would flash by and I'd think it was the cops. I'd stop breathing. I'd hold my breath till they passed. I was holding my breath more times than I wasn't.

Then my cellphone rang. I looked at the clock. Three in the morning. "Hello?" It was Lisa. I told her to stop crying. "Just stop crying and tell me what's the matter." She said she didn't mean to. She said she did it for me and all I could hear was Lisa crying on the other end. She'd told the sergeant on me. She'd ratted me out. She kept on blubbering about choices and making hard choices and I shouted, "You don't think this was a hard choice?!" and I hung up on her.

I looked and saw a dead deer lying up ahead on the road. It looked like a truck'd run right over its head. I tried looking for its eyes; I do that, I look for the eyes in roadkill… "They're going to hunt you down." I was looking in its eyes. "And they're gonna find you and they're gonna destroy you." Hunt you down like an animal, and I got to thinking they were like a wolf, like they were like this wolf chasing me, their mouths all full of rabies and I was running and it was just there, just behind me in the darkness and if I stopped for just a second it would jump on top of me and rip me to shreds, and I got to a stop sign in the middle of the highway and I just started screaming! I was just sitting there at the stop sign, no cars in sight, just screaming.

And then my phone wouldn't stop ringing. First from my sergeant; he was so mad I thought he was going to bite my head off like a chicken. He said, "Git your ass back here, Private James." Then he said he'd kick my ass. And then he said my ass was grass. And you know what I said to him? "If you like my ass so much, why don't you try licking it, Sarge?!" And then I hung up! Can you believe that?! I mean I never done a brave thing in my whole life before that. I started laughing. Like I'd gone crazy or something. Just then my headlights hit the big green sign for Ohio and I get another call, this time from the general. The friggin' general! And he starts playing all good cop with me, saying that he understands people make mistakes and I just turn off my phone and crank up Biggie.

After a while the sun started coming up and my eyes were just burning. I had this fever I swore would split my head from ear to ear. Just crack it right open like an egg. The windows started fogging. Towns started flicking past: Slabtown, Beaverdam, Bluffton, Rawson... When I opened my eyes I was at a truck stop. I couldn't remember how I got there. I tried looking at the licence plates to figure out where I was. Michigan. I looked around... made sure nobody saw me sitting there, slumped at the wheel. I pulled back out onto the road and made it past Toledo and right up alongside that big friggin' lake into Detroit. Just a big city of turnpikes. I headed over the bridge and into Windsor and then I remembered the border. Like I'm serious, I actually forgot all about the border and all the checkpoints and stuff. Thought I'd just keep driving until it got cold and snowy and I'd know I was in Canada. I drove up and told the woman I was going to visit friends in Toronto. And she let me through! And you know what I did? The second I got over I jumped out at the friggin' tourist attraction or whatever and I danced! I'm serious, like I did this little dance and I was just laughing and laughing and laughing; people must've thought I'd lost my mind.

And I just kept driving, up past Guelph and Kitchenette and Toronto, and I would've stayed in Toronto but I got there real late at night and I got mugged so I said "screw this" and kept on going. And I was driving around and around Kingston for like two hours looking for a pawnshop, you know, so maybe I could sell my TV or something for some gas money, but they didn't have one! So of course I ran out. In some crap part of town, nothing but warehouses all around. And I was just like sitting there on the side of the road feeling like

an idiot, you know. Like worthless. I listened to the radio. I listened
to it until the truck battery died. And I sat there crying, the sky
getting dark. Frig. I watched some crows doing something over on
some power lines. Friggin' crows. They started circling above the
truck. Just circling and circling like I was dead or something and
they were just waiting to swoop down and eat up my carcass and I
started shouting, "I ain't dead yet, you stupid birds!"

And that's when I remembered that email. That email from Barry
Winchell's friend.

I jumped outta the truck and started running, looking for like an
Internet café or a library or even someone with one of those friggin'
BlackBerrys or whatever. And if you thought finding a pawnshop
in Kingston was hard, I looked for three hours before I found this
dingy little place. I called the number in the email and this woman
answered. It sounded like I woke her up. I told her where I was and
she said she'd send a guy named Joel Hardin to meet me and that I
was to meet Joel Hardin at the Tim Hortons. I had no idea what a
Tim Hortons was. You know what I thought? I thought it was like
a furniture store. So I hung up the phone and just started running.
It was raining real hard at this point and I was shivering. And I still
had that fever cutting through me. I ran till I thought my heart was
like going to blow up or something and I was shaking. What if Joel
got there and I wasn't there? I ran a half-hour straight till I found
it. I ran in and it was empty. Second I stopped moving I felt like I
was gonna throw up. I ran to the washroom but before I got to the
toilet I blew all over the stall. I just started dry-heavin' and pulling
out all this toilet paper and cleaning up the mess, and I was crying
thinking Joel'll've already come and gone. And I was crying 'cause
I didn't even have enough money for a doughnut. And what if I'd

gotten the wrong Tim Hortons; I mean why do you people have so many friggin' Tim Hortons!? How many doughnuts do you people need?! I stood up, all shaking, spittle on my face, shirt all caked in puke, and I walked outta the washroom and there was a man standing there. In a leather jacket. Nice eyes. He had really nice eyes. I walked up to him and he handed me a doughnut. It was a really nice doughnut. And he just kept saying over and over, "I'm not a cop, I'm not a cop." I looked into his eyes. He could see I'd been crying. And I said, "You're like... the lesbian underground railroad." And then I threw up all over him.

SKYLER *crouches down, her back against the door.*

You know what I'm going to say, don't you?

Pause.

They want to send me back.

Beat.

But I'm going to fight them. You never met a tougher girl than me, Budgie. And I can do this alone... But I'd rather do it with you.

Beat.

Come on, Becca, I know I ain't been square with you but I'm putting it all out there now; I mean, this is it!

Pause.

That woman who keeps calling the apartment? Colleen? She ain't my aunt. She's my lawyer. Joel set me up with her. She says it's gonna be an uphill battle. Well, 'cause we don't have those notes. But how was I supposed to know to keep 'em? I wasn't thinking ahead. Second I'd get one I'd just crumple it up and throw it away. Well wouldn't you? She kept grillin' me about them; she told me if there was a single hole in my story they'd rip it apart. I mean they'd just rip me to shreds. She said she wasn't gonna have me make a fool of her, that this was a high-profile case and our story had to be airtight. She just like friggin' dragged me through the coals, Becca. Four hours, five hours, six hours, over and over. "Where are they?" "How many were there?" "What did they say?" "That's not what you said the first time." And then all of a sudden she leans back in her chair and says, "There weren't any notes, were there?!" And I just snapped. I mean I slammed my hands down on the desk and shouted, "Even if I was lying, okay, even if I made up the notes, does it matter? I mean, even if I was lying, it was so bad, it was just the friggin' worst; you have *no idea* what it's like to be hated like that, you have no *friggin'* idea." That's when she closed my file. She said we were all done for the day. "Wait! I guess what I'm trying to say... is like... even if they didn't write those notes... which *they did*... But like even if they didn't, they said those things, they thought 'em, they... you know, like... all the time too, not even a little bit of the time, it was like *all* the time. Okay? So you don't know." And I started crying. "There were notes, there were, every single day; I lost count there were so many!"

Beat.

What do you do when your own lawyer don't believe you? I told the story so many times over... gets to the point where I don't even believe myself.

I just wish things could get normal again, you know? I mean I'm normal. I think sometimes I'm like the most normal girl in the world: not skinny, not fat, not tall, not short, not pretty, not ugly, not smart but not too dumb… When the cops were looking for me I bet they asked the sergeant, like, "What's she look like?" and he'd say, "Real normal. Like the most normal looking girl you ever met."

SKYLER *walks back over to the door, pressing her hands and forehead against it. She whispers to Rebecca through the door.*

Budgie, every time I come home, and I look around our apartment, I look at those chairs we bought from Ikea that we put together ourselves, and we were laughing at all their silly Swedish names… I mean who names furniture?! It's crazy! And I look at the paint on the walls… We chose that paint. Midnight Plum. Summer Blush. Willow Breeze. Like porn-star names! And then we got cats! I mean we like have cats! You know?

Beat.

There are things you say… there are ways you say it… that open up like these… windows… in my head. Things you like do with your hands. The way you like always jiggle the faucet or whatever to get the water to stop dripping, even though it *never* does. I even like the way you fart; I'm serious. I love it. Hey.

Beat.

You crying? Ain't no reason to cry. I ain't gonna let them send me away. You hear me? I said I ain't gonna let it happen!

Beat.

Why you crying?! Why aren't you saying nothing? Why won't you let me in!? *Let me in*! Don't you get it, Budgie!? It's you!

You're my home.

What am I supposed to do?

The door to the bathroom unlocks.

Blackout.

End of play.

Postscript: After a lengthy legal battle, Skyler finally won the right to remain legally in Canada in 2011. The American military's Don't Ask, Don't Tell Policy was repealed a year later. At the time of publication, Skyler was engaged to be married to her girlfriend.

rihannaboi95

On Being Sunny
by Owais Lightwala

In the early days of rehearsal, director Zack Russell and I talked a lot about whether *rihannaboi95* was closer to film or theatre and what the difference would mean for the performance. On one hand, it's quite clearly a film. There is a camera. There is no immediate audience. The performance required me to internalize much of the range of Sunny's emotions, since the camera is so close to me it amplifies every little gesture and movement exponentially. That said, it's also clearly a piece of theatre. The entire piece is performed and experienced in real time. The performance is live and shot in a single take covering the entire story from beginning to end. There are multiple runs of the show, and with each one a different performance that can only be experienced by that night's audience. Sunny's own awareness of the webcam comes and goes, complicating his relationship with this silent window to the outside world.

So what does that make it? A live film? Or intermedia theatre?

We could only agree that it was a combination of both, and ultimately the question became about how best to tell the story at hand.

Through the rehearsals and the week-long run, I think the biggest challenge for me was learning how to work with the "aloneness." Whether it's a stage with a packed audience or a film set with just the cameraman and a handful of crew around, there has always been someone present in the room, energies that feed my work as an actor. Being shut in this tiny bedroom completely by myself, I thought a lot about what it means to be alone. Not just physically alone, but emotionally alone, as Sunny feels a growing distance between himself and everyone else in his world. The claustrophobic intimacy of the bedroom reinforced that feeling for me, that feeling of isolation and distance that allows a certain vulnerability that we have a hard time accessing in public social situations. The irony, of course, is that in that moment of complete vulnerability and openness, Sunny is actually broadcasting to the whole world. It speaks directly to our times and to how the Internet has changed the way we think about the meaning of privacy and the personal, where everyone can be watching while no one is.

In the end, I think Sunny's anguish and loneliness resonates so strongly because, even in our hyper-connected age, we are all alone on some level. On some level we are all looking for someone to see us as we are—love us or hate us, but *see* us. I feel incredibly fortunate to have been invited to join this piece's journey. Maybe I'm biased, but I'm sure you'll find Sunny as rich, complex, moving, and fascinating as I have.

rihannaboi95 was first produced by Suburban Beast from April 23 to 28, 2013. The play was performed nightly in a bedroom and live-streamed over the Internet for audiences to watch from their computers. It featured the following cast and crew:

Performed by Owais Lightwala
Directed by Zack Russell
Production and production design by Naomi Skwarna

This play was originally commissioned by and first developed with the financial support of Project: Humanity.

rihannaboi95 was nominated for three Dora Mavor Moore Awards in 2013, and won Best New Play in the Theatre for Young Audiences division.

rihannaboi95 is meant to be performed as a YouTube confessional video (a direct-address monologue to a webcam).

Toronto, 2013. A teenage girl's bedroom in an inner suburban apartment.

SUNNY, a sixteen-year-old boy, begins speaking to us.

SUNNY
Ya, YouTube, it's me, rihannaboi95, a.k.a. humble in the jungle. By the time I upload this, by the time you see this, not sure where I'll be. Hopefully things won't be any worse than they are now.

Thanks for liking my "Single Ladies," it has like three thousand views and ninety-four likes, so xoxo ya'll for that. That's made things, you know, a little better…

He points to his lip.

You see this? Ouch. Yeah, shit's got pretty heavy today. I'm hiding here until they come for me. I don't know for how much time. I know I don't talk in my videos normally but this might be my last one for a while. And I know there's a lot of haters out there, posting shit like, "Only thing better than a dancing fag is a dead fag," or whatever, but there's like a hundred people out there who give me the thumbs up, you know, saying "Beyoncé would be proud" or "You're so fierce," so I ain't got time for haters. I make these videos for you—whoever you are—watching in your bedrooms with the volume low down, or on your headphones, under your covers. I love you. And I need you tonight. More than ever. And if you've got like some advice for me, just post it below this video, okay?

Some of you are probably like, "rihannaboi, where'd you get those nice posters, where'd you get those, um, those nice bedsheets?"

He picks up his laptop and revolves it to show the room.

So this is my friend Keira's room. She's giving me some privacy right now. Her light is like phosphorescent or whatever so it makes my skin look all yellow on here. Actually, shit, I shouldn't say her name— So my friend, she says I never smile. And that I talk all quiet. Well duh. Back on Replin Road? Shit, gurl, I'm a *bhadwe ki nasal*. Boys in Rocawear sweatsuits shout, "*Chaaka*! Faggot!" And you wonder why I never smile? And I talk quiet 'cause my family's apartment is like this big.

He indicates a tiny size with his fingers.

You know, when I'm dancing in my videos I'm not even playing any music 'cause the kitchen's right on the other side of the door. So what I do is I listen to a song over and over again at night on ear-buds, going through the moves in my head. And then when I make the videos I do all the moves and put the song in afterwards and it synchs up perfect. I just make sure Mom's on the phone or Dad has the TV up high. Yeah so I don't smile—

"Sunny, you're a girl-boy," "Don't stand like that, don't talk like that, you embarrass us," "Be a man," "Be more like King"— My brother King runs the Koodo Mobile at Lawrence Square. Girls like his big watch and his Sean Johns and they let him fuck them between shifts and he blows all his money on nice clothes. I'm like a bad smell in the room everyone tries to ignore. Neighbours come by and ask how we are and mom and dad talk about the whole family—uncles and aunties back home—they talk about the fucking silverfish in the bathtub before they talk about me. Most of the time I slip their mind. That's what my mom says: "Oh you just slipped my mind," like it was my fault or something. "Well you shouldn't sit in the corner!" "*Acha*, don't be such a baby, you don't hear King whining like this!"

There's a knock at the door. SUNNY freezes. He goes to the door and opens it. He can be heard off-camera saying:

Yeah I'm okay. Yeah. No. I'm not hungry. Okay.

He returns to the computer.

Oh my god, my heart was skipping like so much. So yeah, this isn't my computer. All my problems began when our computer broke. Well, it didn't break; my brother King just put his fist through it when he was talking to his girl Alicia. She can piss him off bad sometimes.

But it was the week I had a big assignment due. Dad said he'd pick up a new one as soon as he could.

But yeah, so I got this big assignment in Civics and Careers from Mr. Bailey, who King thinks is a total gangsta. That first time Bailey walked into class—you should have seen him: black dress shirt, grey slacks, black dress shoes, like Denzel fucking Washington; a bit of grey on the sides, a perfect trimmed beard. He spoke like a TV doctor, you know, using words like "regression" and "undocumented." He looked around the classroom and our eyes locked. And all of a sudden I imagined him standing in front of his bathroom mirror, shirtless, his head tilted, trimming each hair on his chin with a pair of silver scissors, snip, snip, snip. And like I was in the back of the class melting under my hoodie, just a baggy pile of clothes on my seat.

So anyway Bailey gave us this assignment where we had to write a response on a current news event? And people were going on about the economy and Obama and school shootings and stuff and then I put up my hand and I was like, "What about Rihanna and Chris Brown?" And people laughed. But I was serious. I mean, here's like the biggest pop star, this independent-minded woman, you know, and she's beaten black and blue by this guy and then she ends up getting back together with him and like... I don't know, I rambled on about role models for young women and I could see Mr. Bailey nodding at the front of the room and when I finished he was just like, "Excellent."

But my computer's broken, right, and all assignments have to be typed, so I went up to him after class and he suggested the library, and I told him it closed at six and that it took me like fifty minutes to get there by bus so that only left me like half an hour to write anything. He thought for a second and then took this laptop outta his desk. "Here," he said. I'm like, "For real?" He told me it's his spare one—he just uses it for school work. He's like, "Just log into the guest account and bring it back when you're done."

So like what would you do if you got your teacher's laptop? Try to hack into his account, right? Like duh. I'm like sitting on my bed trying to figure out his password but I can't, so, fine, I just log into the guest account and start writing my stupid essay, writing shit like, "By not speaking out against domestic violence and by returning to a relationship with Chris Brown, blah, blah," and I was getting bored so I started watching some Rihanna videos, you know, for like research or whatever. God she's so sexy. King says he wants to fuck her but I just want to watch her, learn her, be her. I played the videos over and over. And then I started doing some of her moves. Trying to figure out how she does it. But I needed an umbrella, right, and my mom has one in her closet so I'm like—"For real, should I grab it? Nah, that's crazy." But man, something in me was pulling me so strong. I crept quiet 'cross the kitchen to her room, creaked open her door, slipped in, tiptoed to her closet, reached around in the dark till I felt it, and grabbed it and snuck back to my room, and it was like the best, holding that umbrella, twirling it just like Rihanna does.

And then I heard my mom get up to go to the bathroom and I started clicking like crazy to mute the video, but I turned on the laptop's camera by accident. Shit. There I was. And the music's still playing... and it's like I was in the video. I hit record and I did all of "Umbrella," start to finish, like perfect, just like Rihanna does. And after I was done I watched myself over and over and my heart was like racing. It was kinda embarrassing but also so... good. Like

I mean, *wallahi* I looked so good. Sexy. Like a real dancer. And for some reason I wanted Mr. Bailey to see me like this. To understand something about me. That I was more than just some student in his class. That I was like an adult—on his level.

When he was collecting the assignments the next day my stomach knotted so bad; I couldn't show him the video, and when he came to me I was just like, "I didn't do it." He looked disappointed. "I need it tomorrow or it's a zero." What would he say when he saw it? Would he tell my parents? tell King? show his grade twelve World Religions class: "Look students, an example of *haram*: a dancing faggot"? When the bell rung I walked up to his desk, and like I noticed the Queen's master's degree framed above it; I'm very observant that way. He was wiping down the chalkboard and his blazer was all covered in white dust and he was saying at Montessori they had whiteboards when I blurted out, "I did it, I did the assignment, and actually I decided to make a movie as my response." He was like, "A movie?"

My hands were all sweaty and I pressed play and bumped up the volume. He turned it down a bit but I could tell he was liking it; he was smiling and nodding. And when it finished we just sat there for a few seconds and then he was like, "Very creative." He asked me why I chose to "embody" Rihanna and I just shrugged, like I wasn't even really sure what he meant. He said it looked like a labour of love and I said, "Yes, it was." And then, I don't know why, but I told him that sometimes I dream about making movies when I grow up. Like music videos or even ones for the Cineplex. He made a face like this *(makes the face)*, like he was thinking hard, and then said his husband Paul is a filmmaker who makes documentaries about drinking water or some shit, but I'm like not even listening, like my mind was racing like—"Husband? Husband?" Like what the fuck, right?

"I'd rather you keep that between us." He said he prefers to keep certain things private from his students—and I'm like still trying to, like, process what's going on, 'cause like I'd never met a gay person before, and suddenly I didn't know how I felt about him and I thought about King and what he'd say if he knew Mr. Bailey was a fag, but then I realized he's still talking, talking about how he's been trying to start a media program at the school ever since he arrived but how there's no money. "Listen, Sunny, I still need you to write the assignment, but I want you to keep making videos, okay? I might be able to count them as extra credit. Be creative." He asked me what I thought about that and I was like, "Yeah, I think that sounds cool."

He told me it's important as an artist that I always follow my creative impulses or whatever. He showed me how to edit my videos using this program, like how to cut things up and move them around and add colour. And he said, you know, it's important to have inspiration or whatever, like to watch the work of other artists if you want to get better. I told him I'm not an artist but he started showing me some videos on YouTube—like this weird dance video and, um, some music videos by the guy who did that *Eternal Sunshine* movie and just like a bunch of arty stuff. You know the kind of stuff I'm talking about, right? Weird costumes and shit?

And then I realized it was four forty-five, and I was like, "Shit, I've totally missed my bus." I told him I lived on Replin Road and that the next bus didn't come for like an hour. He told me he could give me a lift and I was like—"Shit yeah!" Well actually I just nodded, keeping it cool, and I waited for him to pack up his papers and another teacher came by and they chatted for a bit and then we walked out to the parking lot and over to his white Honda. And I made to get into the back seat 'cause I was trying to be polite and he was laughing like, "What do you think this is, a taxi?" So I climbed into the front and his Honda still had that like new-car smell. He turned the key and the radio came on and we were driving down Allen Road when Rihanna started playing and he turned it up and I could hear him listening to me listen to the song and I was listening to him listening to me and suddenly I felt like I fucking *was* the only girl in the world, his only student, and this was the only car, and it didn't even feel like we were driving but that we were flying through apartments, over houses, or maybe we were on a road trip and would leave the city behind forever…

SUNNY *turns on the song and we watch him, in his reverie, ride in Mr. Bailey's Honda down the road.*

And then, shit, I looked up and we were at the top of Replin and I was thanking him and he was waving goodbye and driving away and I watched his car disappear towards the highway, a little speck into night.

And I couldn't move. And I couldn't go home, so I walked to the mall, my head all spinning, and visited King at Koodo, and I was about to tell him about Mr. Bailey, how his favourite teacher was a fag, just to see what he'd say, like maybe he wouldn't even care—but I was too scared. So I didn't. We were grabbing milkshakes at the Burger King when "Only Girl (In the World)" came on again and suddenly it was like I was right back in that car and Mr. Bailey's sitting right beside me driving down Allen Road. King was like, "What's wrong?"—said I dazed out—and I just shook my head. Told him I was tired. And the whole week was like that. I'd hear the song playing in someone's apartment or in Future Shop and I'd be back in that Honda, or sometimes right inside Rihanna's music video, in the middle of the desert, surrounded by flowers, fireworks going off behind me. Each night under the covers I'd watch it, over and over, studying each move, getting the arms so specific, so perfect.

And I kept finding myself doing them as I was walking home or in the shower, the song playing over and over, and I'm singing it right to Mr. Bailey, sitting in his car, at his desk, in his living room, drinking wine with Paul on their leather couch, listening to classical music in their Christian Lacroix turtlenecks, as he drew the regions of Palestinian occupation on the overhead projector and wiped chalk dust from the board...

You have no idea how hard it was to make a video in my apartment, everyone living on top of each other, King always getting up in my bidness. So I had to plan it out. The only time my family left the apartment was Saturdays when we visited Auntie, who's like not even my real auntie but some old family friend, and we always had to go once a week. So like that morning I pretended I was sick, soup can into the toilet, you know, so Mom let me sleep when they went. The second they left I jumped outta bed 'cause I knew I only had like two hours. I set the laptop up in front of the bathtub 'cause we have this shower curtain with all these flowers on it that look kinda like the ones from Rihanna's video and, like, if I leaned back on the curtain like this it looked like I was lying back on the flowers like she did. And I strung these blinking Christmas lights I got from Dollarama along the curtain rod to be the fireworks and wrapped our tablecloth around me and put on this headband and used half of Mom's lipstick until it was so thick I thought my lips would collapse. And I'd watched the video so many times that I had it memorized. I pressed record, climbed into the tub, and began singing to it in my head and doing the moves, exactly like Rihanna did, like so specific, singing right to Mr. Bailey in his car.

And suddenly there's banging on the door. I slipped back and grabbed the curtain rod but it gave out and I smashed my head against the fucking tiles, all the Christmas lights falling on me. I heard King's voice: "I need to piss." And I just yanked the shower on and shouted, "I'm in the shower!" He said, "I need to go, unlock the door." I felt blood all over the back of my head and the smashed lights cutting my back. I unplugged them so I wouldn't fry myself and pulled off the white cloth and tried rubbing the lipstick off but it just smudged all over my face. "One second!" I stumbled out of the shower and stuffed the laptop under the sink and tried fixing the curtain rod back into place but King was pounding on the door now. "What are you doing in there, jerking off?" I got the curtain back up and flicked open the lock and jumped back behind the curtain, my feet landing on the smashed lights. I bit my lip, like *wallahi* so much pain. I heard King over by the toilet beginning to piss. "What happened to the curtain?" he said. "You were rushing me, I slipped." I watched my blood swirling down the drain as I was trying not to cry. King walked over to the sink and said, "What's Mom's lipstick doing here?" My heart jumped into my throat. The lipstick. Fuck. I pretended not to hear. "Sunny?" My eyes were closed, I said nothing. "Make sure you fix that curtain, okay?" And then he left.

But you've all seen that video—I nailed it, right? Well like I cut out the part where I slip and shit—that's why it ends so sudden. I stayed up all night editing it under my covers and showed up the next day to Mr. Bailey's class before the bell. He was sitting by himself with his Starbucks latte and *Globe and Mail*. He waved me in and we sat down at his desk and watched the video.

The opening strains of Rihanna's "Only Girl (In the World)" start to play. SUNNY *sings along to some of the lyrics.*

He said he always thinks she says "hot guy" instead of "hot ride" and we laughed and he had his hand at his mouth like this, like he was looking at a painting in the fucking Louvre, and it made me feel, like, so amazing. And when it was done he said, "It's beautiful." He called it beautiful. Or maybe he meant I was beautiful.

And then he took out this pamphlet from his desk for something called the Queer Youth Video Project or whatever and he was talking about how I should check it out and I suddenly got all hot in the face like he'd slapped me and I said, "I'm not a queer." I didn't mean to shout it but I did. He stopped and looked at me. He put his hand on my shoulder and I shrugged it off and said, "I'm not a queer." I was so angry but I knew I shouldn't be, like I knew I was being stupid and I didn't know what to do so I just ran to the bathroom and I was crying like a faggot, like a girl, and I didn't even care if people saw me; fuck them, fuck all of them. I splashed cold water on my face. I looked at myself in the mirror, like this.

SUNNY *does the look.*

Very movie-like, very dramatic. The bell rang and I looked down and realized I was still holding the laptop. I was too embarrassed to go back to class so I just walked all the way home—past the strip mall and the highway and the bungalows all the way back to Replin, up the stairs two at a time, past Dad sleeping on the couch, rattling the cupboards with his snores, and not even waking up to the sound of me puking in the toilet, this time for real.

For the rest of the week I didn't look Mr. Bailey in the eye. I'd sit at the back of the class, pull my Sean Jean over my head, slouch low. I didn't put my hand up, and he kept his distance too, so fine. Cool. But

I kept making videos. Like every night. Sometimes two a night. Had to do it quiet, like when Dad and King were watching soccer or talkin' with Grannie back home on speakerphone, and I'd be in my bedroom doing the moves silent, like no noise, all the songs memorized, cutting it all together afterwards under my covers. But the thing was—I wanted y'all to see them. To know, you know. To watch like Mr. Bailey did, his hands at his face like he was looking at a fucking Michelangelo, thinking it was worth something, telling me my moves were good—'cause otherwise I was just some guy dancing alone by himself in his bedroom, you know? Pathetic. Like totally alone. So yeah. That's why I started putting them on YouTube, I guess. That night watching my first video load so slow, one per cent at a time, my heart jumping every time the number went up, knowing someone would see it soon and love it and call it beautiful. Call me beautiful.

And I knew, like, once things got on the Internet they had a life of their own. But I didn't care. It's like I couldn't not do it. And if you wanna blame someone, blame Bailey for encouraging me in the first place, for not telling me to watch out or whatever. Maybe a part of me wanted people to know, for everyone to see me like that, to love me or hate me or punch me or whatever they were going to do; I just wanted it out there, and if they thought it was gay or stupid I didn't care 'cause I knew I looked good.

So I made the account. rihannaboi95. I wanted 97 'cause that's when I was born but it was already taken. And I uploaded eight videos. Then three more the next week. And between classes I'd pull out my laptop in the washroom stall and push refresh to see how many people had watched. Twelve, thirty-four, seventy-eight. Who are you? How did you find me? Of all the millions of things, you clicked on me. Did you watch me all the way through?

Got such a rush from the views going up—I tried to imagine your faces. I tried to imagine your bedrooms. By the weekend "Only Girl (In the World)" had 321 views. That's like more people than my entire building. And the next day it was 459, and the day after that over a thousand. And every time the number went up, every time you gave me a thumbs up or wrote "this is better than the real one" or even when they gave me thumbs down and wrote "I hate fags," "rihanna would be ashamed," it didn't matter because you were watching. 'Cause I was worth watching.

I thought about showing the videos to Mr. Bailey but I was too embarrassed about how I acted when he gave me that pamphlet. Like I knew I wasn't gay, or at least I didn't wanna be, and I kept worrying he'd see something inside of me I didn't want him to and pull it out. But I still thought about him like all the time. One night I took out his laptop from under my bed where I hid it and suddenly I thought about trying to log into his account again. This time when it asked me for a password I typed "P A U L"—and it fucking worked! There was nothing that exciting on there. No porno. Except his background photo—it was full of info. It was a photo of a house, looked just finished like it was in a new suburb or whatever, and there's a man by the curb beside a street sign—an older guy, like in his fifties or something. I couldn't totally read the sign but I think it said "Maplegrove" and the number of the house was fourteen; I could see it if I looked closely beside the door. I typed "14 Maplegrove" into Google Maps and the pin dropped on a winding street in North York, just a few blocks from the mall. Listen, it's not like I was stalking him—I'm a curious person. And for some reason it comforted me to know where he was right then. That he existed outside of that classroom, you know? I stashed his computer back under my bed and lay back and imagined the interiors of his house, the wall-to-wall carpet, the wood trim, the bold red paint in the dining room like the colour of lipstick… which, oh yeah, the next morning I noticed my mom began keeping her's in a different bathroom drawer than usual, like she was totally starting to suspect, even though I only used it in two videos.

So after school that day I got off the bus a few stops early and walked through the Shoppers at Lawrence Square. I walked up and down the makeup aisles making sure no one saw me, or sometimes scrunching up my face like I was some bro buying blush for his girlfriend. When this girl walked up to me—said Keira on her name tag. And she just picked up some foundation and handed it to me like, "This one would work best for your skin tone." And she gently grabbed my hand, brought it up like this, and brushed some of it on. *(SUNNY does this for the camera.)* And it blended in perfect. "See?" she said. I swallowed. I told her I was doing Nicki Minaj for Halloween. For a joke. She was like, "Okay, well you'll need some fake lashes. And eyeliner and lip gloss," and she just began picking it off the shelf like she was doing groceries. But when I got to the cash she looked at me and was like, "Do you have an older brother?" I was like, "Uhh yeah." Shitting myself, right? "His name King?" "Yeah." "I used to date him." It was like someone threw a bucket of cold water on me. She told me not to worry—they don't talk anymore. She's like, "He's a douche, no offence," and I was like, "Yeah, that's cool." I told her, "Please don't tell him, okay?" and she's like, "I told you, we don't talk, is cool."

That night King and I were walking through the neighbourhood, the sun coming down red and casting long shadows. We have good walks together, never having to say much. And we stopped to watch some ball on the court when he said, "Saw you met an old girlfriend of mine." I swallowed. "She told you?" He laughed. "Dumb-ass, I saw you became friends on Facebook." But he was chill about it. I told him I liked her—that I wanted to get to know her, and he shrugged and was like, "She's all yours, bro."

I started making the videos longer, better, more moves, pushing harder, but still making no noise, dancing in silence, my family always just on the other side of the door. The better I made them, the more y'all watched, till it was up to like a hundred and fifty a day. I was living this total double life, like a superhero—quiet Sunny in the hoodie at the back of class during the day, no one gives a shit about, and then rihannaboi95, a fierce booty-shaking force of nature with five thousand views. Riding the bus, writing tests, eating dinner, the whole time living a secret under everybody's noses, King's, Mr. Bailey's. At least until today.

Today started normal—breakfast, bus ride—until I get to my locker and these boys, like, five grade-twelve boys come up to me and start dancing right up in my face, acting all gay and doing Rihanna's moves in my face like right from my videos, and they're singing "I'm the only fag in the world," and I feel everything begin to spin. They know. They've seen the videos. How many?—maybe all of them. Good. Fuck them. Watch them all for all I care. I grab my binder and start walking to class when suddenly something hits the back of my head, almost knocks me over. It's a pencil case. I pick it up and throw it back at them, and so, yeah, I've never been a good thrower, and it falls like way short and they just start laughing louder. In class it feels like everyone's looking at me, whispering. Do they all know? How? Whatever, I don't give a shit, three hundred of you gave me the thumbs up, you think I care what they think?—I pull up my hood and slouch lower in my seat.

When the bell rings I run to my locker and there's a condom taped to it. And there's spit in it. Or cum. Maybe real cum. But I just peel it off and throw it on the ground like I don't even see it 'cause I can tell everyone in the hall's watching me, wanting me to react, but I keep cool and undo my lock and take out my laptop and nobody sees I'm crying; I don't want nobody to see so I run into the washroom and I shut myself in the farthest stall and try to connect to the Wi-Fi, even though the washrooms are like fucking cement bunkers and have no reception, but YES finally I do—and Facebook loads so slow but I can already see it: they found the videos and posted them on my wall. And on their walls. And on everyone's wall. Those boys from grade twelve—I think some of them are friends with King. And they've even made a fan page for me, with all my videos on it, guys and their girlfriends and their friends posting sarcastic shit like, "Wow he's such an amazing dancer," and, "Oh wow I would love to have sex with him he's so sexy hmmmmmm fuck my butt faggot." And I punch the wall with my fist and I scream 'cause its concrete and I kick the door again and again until it starts to break off the hinge. Good, let it break. I want it to break.

The bell rings and another bell but I got a lot more crying in me and I let it all out until it's almost the end of the day and I finally climb outta the stall. And I catch myself in the mirror. And I stop. And I look at myself. My puffy eyes, in King's puffy-ass hoodie and jeans—the shadow above my lip, not enough hairs for a moustache, my too-big nose like my dad's. And I can feel Chris Brown pacing outside the bathroom, fists clenched, and I'm leaning over the sink crying and suddenly, *wallahi*, I hear Rihanna whisper in my ear, right here, so soft, she says, "Don't be afraid of them, Sunny, they're just a bunch of boys. They're all just little boys." But I tell her I am, I'm afraid—I say, "Rihanna, don't leave me; I can't do it." And she says, "You just gotta own it, Sunny." But how? How'm I supposed to own it? I look around the bathroom but it's empty. The urinals flush. Rihanna? She's gone. I take another good long look at myself and I know she's right. I just gotta own it. I pull off my hood and I'm gonna strut right back into class and I'm gonna say, "Yeah, you like those videos? I got two more coming this weekend. And you can all subscribe or kiss my ass, don't make no difference to me." And I stuff the laptop back in my bag and swing it over my shoulder and bust out of the washroom—and right into Mr. Bailey.

I ask him how he knew I was in there. He says, "Rihanna told me." He asks me why I wasn't in class and I shrug. Says he overheard some students talking about my videos and I don't say anything. "Sunny, are there videos of you online? Sunny?" "What?" "I asked you a question." "Yeah." "Videos of you dancing? How many?" "A few." "And you posted these on YouTube?" "Yeah." "Why?" "Why should I tell you?" "Because I think you're making yourself a target." And this gets me so mad. I tell him I'm expressing myself and that he's the one who told me to follow my creative impulses, and he's like, "Listen, this is a tough school and there're lots of people out there who don't get it." "So? I should change myself for them? I don't give a shit if they don't get me." Except I don't say "shit" and I mutter it 'cause I'm trying not to cry, and then he says it again, that I'm making myself a target if I'm posting my videos and I'm like, "What the hell's the point of making art if you can't even show it to anyone? All those videos you showed me by all those old white guys were on YouTube. Are they making themselves targets?" He rubs his head, frustrated, and brings his voice down low and quiet and he's like, "Sunny, are you making these videos with the laptop I lent you?" I shrug. "You broke my trust, Sunny—that was not what we agreed you would use it for. Did you stop to think about the position that puts me in?" He says if this blows up—if my parents call the school—they'll ask where I got the laptop and that puts him in an "extremely compromising position," which actually sounds kinda hot. "I have to ask you to give me back the computer, Sunny." "No. You can't. It's all I got." And I turn and just start to run, full tilt down the hall, Mr. Bailey calling after me, but I'm too fast to catch, he hasn't got a chance. I run right out of the school, through the strip mall parking lot, past apartments full of people, people in Jungle just wanting a break and just getting broken. It takes me a long time to get home. I take the longest route back I can.

And when I finally do it's dark and Mom, Dad, King, and two of our neighbours are all sitting at the kitchen table like they've been waiting for me. Mom's been crying. "Sorry," I say. "I decided to walk home." Then I see a laptop on the table opened to YouTube and King pushes play and I begin to dance, on the screen, Mom's umbrella in my hand. She starts to moan, says I've brought shame on them all. Suddenly Dad grabs me and begins pushing me down into the ground, hitting my head with his hand until I see blood on the tiles, right beside the stains that never come out, no matter how hard Mom scrubs, and the neighbours are pulling him off of me, and Mom's screaming for us to stop when King grabs me and hauls me into the bedroom and locks the door and just begins to cry. And I'm like stunned, like I've never seen him cry before. Not even when we were kids. And he sits down on the bed and he's like, "Why'd you have to go and do this, Sunny? So fucking stupid, man, so fucking stupid..." And he starts to tell me how his friends've been beating on him for it, calling him a fag, and to get them to stop he said he's gonna help them put me in line, put me in my place—"They're gonna come for you, man." "Tonight?" "Yeah tonight." "To the apartment?" And I'm like, "Why they gotta hate so much, it's not like anyone's forcing them to watch the fucking videos," but he's like, "You don't get it, Sunny: it's about the block, Serb, Bengali, Somali, all these guys, we're brothers, it's how the other blocks see us, our family, and you can't go disgracing us like this, dancing like a faggot on YouTube. You don't think about our honour? Didn't you even stop to fucking think, guy? *Wallahi*, so stupid."

I ask him again if they're coming for me for real tonight and he nods and I'm like how many and he's like seven or eight and he tells me I should make a run for it maybe, but I'm already packing up, sticking my laptop in my bag, when he's like, "Shit, guy, where'd you get that MacBook?" My heart drops. I let my guard down. "Yo, let me see that," and he grabs it from me. "This is what you've been making these videos with? I ain't had a computer all month and you've been playing with this?" He tries to open it but I grab it back and we start pulling on it until I kick him hard, with all that I've got, right in the chest like fucking *Mortal Kombat*, and he slams back into the door and my mom starts screaming on the other side and I don't even think, I just jump—right out the window.

Falling two storeys is like… forever. Like I'll keep falling forever. But I smash into a pile of smelly-ass plastic bags, right in the dumpster, and fuck up my ankle; I know the second I land I fucked my ankle, but I don't got any time to worry about that. I reach up for the edge of the dumpster and pull myself outta the garbage and jump down and just start running, best I can with my ankle, just running away with nothing but the laptop and the stink still on me, just running…

I don't even remember getting on the subway and getting off at North York and walking past the mall, down Elmhurst and Bangor until I'm standing in the photograph, on the front steps of 14 Maplegrove Way. I ring the bell and the front lights flick on and it's Paul who answers. Pulls open their fancy glass front door. "Hello?" "It's um… I'm looking for Mr. Bailey. It's Sunny." Paul looks younger in person. Maybe it's the light. He's not squinting against the sun. He calls, "Ben! It's for you!" And he invites me to come inside. It's whiter than I imagined: white walls, grey paintings, white bookshelves, hardwood floors, not carpet, a curving staircase, which I see Mr. Bailey starting to walk down in pyjama pants and a *Walrus Magazine* T-shirt. "Sunny? What on earth are you doing here?" I can't remember what I say. Maybe I just start to cry. "How did you find my house?" I hold up his computer. He bends down beside me: "Are you hurt—did someone try to hurt you?" I tell him they're coming for me. He asks who and I say, "Some guys, some friends of King's. From school. And the block. They want to teach me a lesson." He tells me he's going to call the police and I'm like, "No! Please—don't. It'll ruin everything." But he's already picking up the phone and I shout, "You can't call the police, they'll bring my family into it, the neighbours, and then the block; everyone will be after them, after King, the guys will beat the shit out of him, don't you get it?" I don't know if he did but he put down the phone.

I tell him I just want to stay—maybe even just overnight on his couch—but he's shaking his head: "I can't do that, Sunny. I want to help you but I can't do that." And I ask what about just one night until it all blows over. I tell him I don't have anybody else, but he's still shaking his head, talking about liability, about teacher-student protocol, and I just scream, "Well fuck you too," and run out and slam the door and he pulls it back open and calls, "Sunny!" And I turn around on his front walk. All those perfectly laid stones. "What?" He points to the laptop under my arm. "I need you to give that back to me." And I blow like a volcano and I chuck the laptop at him as hard as I can and so, yeah, I've never been a good thrower, and it falls like way short and explodes on his perfectly laid stone walkway. And we stand there in silence. And then I'm just like, "There. No more videos."

And I start running again—into the dark of his backyard, over the fence, through the next backyard, through sprinklers, and over another fence, until I catch up with a bus and ride it through the neighbourhoods, my eyes closed, rocking back and forth, thinking as long as I stay in motion they can't catch me; maybe I can keep moving my whole life, there's nothing weighing me down no more, nothing at all. 'Course the fucking bus takes me right back to where I came from, last stop Lawrence Square, which I take as a sign, 'cause the only thing open twenty-four hours there is the Shoppers. And I run in and ask for Keira, Keira the makeup girl, but they say I just missed her, that she just left for the night, and I run out into the food court but it's all closed up so I run out to the bus stop and I see her, Keira! with her headphones on waiting for the 116, and I run up to her crying and looking like shit and say, "They're coming for me, you gotta help me. You gotta hide me." And she does. Real gentle—just puts her coat over me like this and says, "Don't worry. I live close." And she doesn't even need to ask any questions 'cause she knows. She knows.

So I'm here—fugitive-style. Making this video on her computer. Any advice y'all have—please—post below. Lemme know what I should do. I'm in a fucking rock and a hard space or whatever the saying is. Mr. Bailey, if you're watching this: I'm sorry. I really am. You're not a bad guy, you did your best. And King, if you're watching this—I want you to know that—

A commotion is heard on the other side of the door. Shouting. Have they come for him? SUNNY *turns off the light and begins to whisper into the camera, illuminated only by the screen.*

It's fucking Chris Brown; he's here for me but I ain't gonna let him touch me. I'm gonna be strong. I'm gonna live tonight. I'm gonna live. And one day I'm gonna go back to Replin Road and I'm gonna walk down the block with no shame, my head held high, shouting "I'm alive, I'm alive, rihannaboi95," and it'd be like a music video with fireworks and a sick beat, and the boys kicking balls against the wall will stop and they'll say, "Shit, look at Sunny." And the dog who no one owns, caught in the stairwell, will stop barking and watch me too. And all the faces in all the apartments, they'll watch. My mom and dad and King and my uncles, faces pressed to the glass. In the middle of Replin I'll hit each move perfect, the music blasting, tight jeans, big hair, low-cut, own it, serve it—they'll be watching me in every apartment and basketball court and car on Allen Road; every shopper in Lawrence Square, every quiet house in the 'burbs, every lonely teen on the bus at night with their heads on the window or watching YouTube under the covers; we're not faggots, we're weapons cocked and fully loaded—we're alive, we're alive, rihannaboi95.

They're in the other room. I can hear them on the other side of the door. Maybe Mom, Dad, King. Maybe Mr. Bailey. All the riders of the 116. Maybe the entire block. All of YouTube…

SUNNY *gets up from the desk, turns the light back on, and begins to blast a Rihanna song—"Where Have You Been." He dances to it brashly—he gives it his all. The door behind him is flung open. From the angle of the camera we do not see who is standing in the next room watching—presumably his family.* SUNNY *keeps dancing. He pays no attention to the open door. When the song concludes he stands still for a moment and then walks over to the computer and turns off the camera.*

End of play.

Peter Fechter:
59 Minutes

On Being Peter
by Jordan Tannahill

I went to Germany to find the real Peter Fechter. I visited the street he lived on in the Weissensee district; I pored over accounts and photographs of the fateful events of August 17, 1962; I read the transcripts from the 1990 trial of the two guards who shot him; and I wept at the memorial erected at the site of his death on Zimmerstrasse. But for all of the museums, archives, and memorials I visited, I came to realize that I would never really find what I was looking for. I would never know what it was like to live in a divided city, I would never know what it was like to risk my life jumping the Wall, and I would never know the real Peter. All I could do was imagine. What would bring me to do what Peter did? How would I have acted in the hours and minutes leading up to carrying it out, and in the final hour spent lying in the Death Strip?

While my research informed my understanding of Peter's world, I realized that I needed to find Peter in myself. I found this quite liberating as a performer. I was not trying to embody the young man in the photograph but rather my own fears and dreams as a young man, my own journey to find love and my place in the world of adults. In this way my performance of Peter in Berlin at the WYE—a short walk from the site of his actual death—was what I would describe as "unaffected and unadorned." I did not attempt to modify my appearance, posture, or voice in any conscious way. Instead, I focused on where the story sat within me and allowed my performance to arise from there.

It was both thrilling and daunting exploring this work in Berlin. I was overwhelmed by the support and interest in the piece, by people's desire to revisit Peter's story, and their openness for a foreigner to find himself in the story. I want this play to be an open invitation for anyone to perform. It's a story that, while innately specific to a time and place in Berlin's history, is a universal allegory and, thus, an enduring one.

Peter Fechter: 59 Minutes was first produced by Suburban Beast from May 10 to 20, 2013, at the WYE in Berlin, Germany. It featured the following cast and creative team:

Performed by Jordan Tannahill
Directed by Christian Barry
Sound design by Richard Feren
Recorded voices performed by Brendan McMurtry-Howlett, David McIlwraith, and Sochi Fried

Cast

Onstage:

Peter, eighteen-year-old male bricklayer

Speaking Roles in Sound Design:

Helmut, nineteen-year-old male bricklayer, Peter's companion
Father, a dentist in his early fifties, Peter's father
Mother, a woman in her early fifties, Peter's mother

Note on Staging

The duration of the performance should be exactly fifty-nine minutes, the length of time the real Peter Fechter lay dying in the Berlin Wall's Death Strip. In our workshop production, a digital clock was projected onto the surface of the stage and the bars of light composing the numbers would recombine to create the locations of the play: halls, rooms, the Death Strip. The performer traversed the physical space of his memory onstage and would then be thrown back into the excruciating present of the Death Strip. The audience was in alley configuration (i.e., on either side of the performer), mirroring the "east/west" spectatorship along the Wall. In the Berlin production, the performer simply stood at a microphone, with only his face illuminated, and spoke the entire text as a digital clock counted down from 59:00 above his head. In both versions we used an intricate sound design in which all other characters were pre-recorded voices. That said, I am not opposed to a director choosing to stage a multi-actor production of the play.

In darkness, PETER *speaks onstage.*

PETER

My mother always told me: never fall asleep with an unanswered question, lest it haunt your dreams.

The sound of a gunshot. It echoes between nearby buildings, birds launch into flight from the adjacent apartment, blood courses through a body. Laboured breathing. A tone, like the sound of a concussion. The digital clock begins to count down from 59:00.

Lights appear on PETER *Fechter, a youth of eighteen.*

It sounded like thunder. Like a storm breaking above our heads. And then all of a sudden my mouth was full of dirt.

I've been shot. No. Yes, I've been shot. Is there pain? Yes. My stomach. Get up. Do it. Move something. Blink. Yes. I can blink. Breathing.

Throat. Can I swallow? No. It hurts. Don't swallow. Right leg. Can I move it? No? Okay. Left leg? No. My weight is on my left leg. Right hand. Yes. Two fingers. I can move two fingers. Now the wrist. I can move the wrist.

One minute and fifteen seconds, I think, "Get up, goddamn it. Don't lie there like a gutted fish, steaming guts on the rock, jump for the ledge!" All you had to do was pull yourself over. But I reached up and his hand wasn't there. Why did I expect it? So stupid: I was waiting for his hand. I replay the moment over in my head:

We're standing at the window.

HELMUT
Are you ready?

PETER
Two storeys above the barbwire fence.

HELMUT
One… two… three!

PETER
We jump.

The sound of both boys jumping from the apartment window into the Death Strip.

…and land on the other side.

The sound of them running. A siren. Shouting of Checkpoint Charlie guards. The sound of PETER's *heavy breathing and pounding heart as he runs; feet on gravel.*

HELMUT
This way, this way!

PETER
The other side seems so far. Much farther than it looked from the window. Every alarm along the Wall, in my body begins to howl; the gravel churns under my feet; run faster, goddamn it, faster! Helmut reaches the other side first. I watch him jump for the top but he misses. He can't reach it. He jumps again and I grab his legs and push him all the way up. And then I reach for his hand. But he's already gone over. He didn't reach down.

The distant sound of the gunshot and its echo.

The gunshot echoes across the Death Strip, between buildings, inside apartments, inside every skull for a dozen square blocks, even birds in mid-flight and they have very tiny skulls.

As I lie there I think: I should have had a cleaner landing, I should have dodged more, jumped faster, jumped harder. Jump from the knees, that's what they said in gym class, not that I ever listened. Mr. Hoffman always said it would get the best of me. I thought he meant cholesterol.

And worse than the bullet, a question begins to burn: "What was worth this?" It seemed clear a moment ago, in the window…

The thing you have to understand is that Helmut had a plan. And time was running out. Every fibre in my body was telling me to go with him, jump, go now, until there was nothing to do *but* jump. Everything was happening so fast I didn't have time to think.

But now I'm too tired. I want to close my eyes but no, "Never fall asleep with an unanswered question." My face in the dirt, whispering "What was worth this?" I can feel the answer lying in the centre of the hole, the red-hot, the part that bleeds, that hurts too much to ahhhhhhhh—need to go to the centre. I take a breath. As slow as I can. My mother would say, "If you cannot find the answer, then perhaps you are not listening close enough." So. I keep very still. And listen.

My body is melting. Like a rotten piece of fruit. I'm slowing down. Slowing to a stop. To the speed of the earth. I try to listen for an answer. I listen as close as I can.

And then… quiet at first…

A thousand ants scuttling in the canals of earth below my ear. If I listen close enough I can hear them. An impossible labyrinth of millions of bodies, all moving as part of an intricate system, a master plan. And the roots of a dandelion four feet away slowly descending, reaching for moisture. A fly passes overhead, each isolated beat of its wings like a helicopter. A bead of sweat slips from my brow, falls silent through the air, and explodes on the gravel like a bomb.

The sound of a heartbeat.

And my heart. Like a war drum. Counting down the seconds, pumping the life right out of me. Pumping blood up my throat. The taste of rusty nails. Of dirt.

The sound of a growling stomach.

And there! The guard is hungry. I can hear his stomach. From where I lie I can hear it in the tower thirty metres away.

The guard's stomach rumbles again.

I listen closer. And his hunger begins to paint a picture. He hasn't eaten breakfast this morning. I see him run through the kitchen on his way to the shower. I see him press the toaster lever, but not hard enough. He returns, towelling off his hair, to two pieces of cold bread and not enough time. Because just then his brother starts honking the horn on his Soviet-made Lada in the street, already irritable at having left his belt at his girlfriend's house, and today of all days being his big presentation to the bankers' association.

And as the brothers drive in silence I can see what they can't: my friend Helmut riding his stolen red bike straight towards the intersection the brothers' car is now converging on. Tired and lost in his thoughts, Helmut careens through the intersection, forcing the brothers to swerve and slam into a parked taxi. Helmut locks eyes with the young guard as he sails past the Lada on his bike. Oblivious that the young guard will begin his tower shift, shaken from the fender-bender and irritable on an empty stomach—so much so that when the Wall is suddenly breached by two would-be defectors only

an hour into his shift, his usually steady aim will give way by fourteen inches as he shoots not the escapee's leg but his lower pelvis.

He points to his own body.

Right here. A cold piece of bread turned into a bullet.

Helmut, meanwhile, takes a back alley and then another to arrive at
my front door for breakfast. We've been walking to build sites every
morning since he got me into bricklaying. My father is no fan of
Helmut and his breakfast visits.

The sounds of a breakfast table.

Helmut joins us at the table, just as Father beings massacring his
second piece of toast with butter.

A sound of knife on toast.

HELMUT
You might be interested to know I cheated death this morning.

PETER
Father doesn't even look up from his toast.

HELMUT
Two cars crashed *this* close to me. Would have been crushed if I
hadn't swerved at the last second.

FATHER
Tell me. Did you drop a loaf of bread in this collision?

HELMUT

What loaf?

FATHER

The bread someone breakfasting in my home every morning for eight months should have the common sense to bring.

PETER

That might've been the most my father had ever said to Helmut. Father always had higher goals for me—like continuing the family dentistry business. As if staring into people's mouths all day was somehow loftier than building homes.

FATHER

But perhaps one too many bricks have fallen on your head.

HELMUT

You're right, sir, many bricks on our heads but unfortunately few coins in our pocket.

FATHER

I suppose if you choose to break your back for a hundred Deutschmarks.

HELMUT

But sir, we don't do it for the Deutschmarks. Our comrades need homes, don't they?

FATHER

If honour is your intention, comrade, then honour your head with a haircut.

Beat.

It confounds me. You intelligent young men romanticizing the pro-
letariat. Does the real world scare you? Or are you content to read
your poems and lay bricks and philosophize? Bricks in your head
more like it.

PETER
My father returns to his toast massacre. He sits hunched, focused,
like a primate learning to use tools. He is a serious man. Always lost
in serious thoughts.

(to FATHER) Is the butter too thick?

FATHER
Less thick than your friend here. I'm trying to make it spread. A little
goes a long way, you know.

HELMUT
Is that why it's rationed?

PETER
I miss the breakfasts Mother used to make. Ham and eggs, maybe
sausage.

FATHER
Breakfast for an early grave.

PETER
I had a dream about her watch last night. Mother's. Do you remember that watch?

FATHER

Hmm?

PETER

Mother's gold watch.

FATHER

Did she have a watch?

PETER

In my dream she's searching empty streets, looking in alleys, in garbage cans, in the gutters, and she's crying because she can't find it anywhere.

Breakfasting sounds; no reply from FATHER.

FATHER

Unlike Rolf to miss breakfast three mornings in a row. Is he sick?

PETER

(to audience) Most mornings we're joined by Rolf, another brick-layer. He's like a duckling: just a dusting of fuzz on his head and a croaking little voice. We're all the same age and became fast friends. He's a self-proclaimed nymphomaniac, even though we'd bet our life he's never even touched a breast. We argue a lot about sex, technique, girls—learned virgins the three of us. And movies and books, we argue about those too. Especially the banned ones. Together we've read more than all the other bricklayers in the city combined. We cast ourselves in different stories. *The Brothers Karamazov. War and Peace.* And the adventures, of course. Victor Hugo. Jules Verne. Jack London. Sometimes we speak in rhyme to

keep something secret from our co-workers. Or quote Nietzsche. Just to drive them crazy.

But Rolf hadn't been to work for the past two days. Just disappeared without a word. And from the circles under his eyes I could tell Helmut was losing sleep over it as much as I was.

FATHER
It's a shame. I always liked him. More sensible than the two of you.

The telephone in the hallway rings.

Excuse me.

FATHER *rises to answer the phone.*

PETER
Father walks into the hall to answer the phone. He hates taking calls at home. Too many ears on the party line. But he's used to choosing his words carefully.

The sounds of FATHER *on the phone; laughing. Faint female voice heard on the other end.*

It's a woman's voice on the other end. Helmut and I watch him from the table. Father leans against the wall, smiling in spite of himself. He looks younger all of a sudden.

FATHER
Are you sure? All right. Hmm, hmm.

PETER

We turn back to our toast as he returns to the table.

FATHER

Just a patient who forgot her umbrella in the clinic. I promised to drop it off on my way to work.

HELMUT

Do all your patients have your home number?

FATHER

There are certain courtesies one extends to women. A bachelor like yourself would be smart to learn them. Poor woman has an apartment only a few metres from the Wall. She finds it impossible to sleep at night on account of the lights. It makes her a fragile sort.

PETER

I can feel Helmut's eyes on me.

A kettle begins to boil in the kitchen.

Father shuffles into the kitchen to retrieve the kettle. He never lifts his feet. Sometimes I hear his feet scraping through the house and think, "Who is this stranger I live with?" More like a cold draft than a man.

HELMUT

(whispers) We have to leave.

PETER

I'm not done my toast.

HELMUT

I mean we have to get over as soon as possible. Today. Rolf is gone.

PETER

Gone where?

HELMUT

I knocked on his door, and just like before: nothing. I was just about to leave when his mother answered. Her eyes were puffy, she looked like hell. I said, "Rolf hasn't been to work in two days." She bit her lip. And shook her head. She said, "Go to work, young man. You'd be best not to ask after him anymore." And that was it. She closed the door.

PETER

(to audience) You have to understand: we had a plan. All of our friends did. Except we were really going to do it. We were to enter the West at the river bend three weeks from now. Every angle was considered, every minute accounted for, each of us with our own specific role.

HELMUT

We have to leave tonight. Today, if possible.

PETER

Are you crazy, how are we supposed to do that?

HELMUT

You think I'm going to just sit around waiting to be caught? He's probably spilling his guts to them—

PETER

(whispers) We had a plan.

HELMUT

Fuck the plan. The plan is done, and so are we if we don't act.

PETER

The river crossing won't work without Rolf. We need three: one for the rope, one for the buoy, one for the bridge.

HELMUT

Forget it: we'll use the apartment.

PETER

What apartment?

HELMUT

Your father's client. You heard him say it: it's smack up against the Wall.

PETER

How?

HELMUT

She just dialed. We call the operator, get her number, and steal your father's address book. Just do a little cross-referencing till we find her. Then we head to the apartment on our way to work. See if it's close enough.

PETER

And break in?

HELMUT

No, we'll just ask her kindly. Of course break in. And jump. If we can. People have done it.

PETER

And what, jump from her window? What if it's on the fifth storey?

HELMUT

I don't know, lower a bedsheet. We can figure it out.

PETER

Besides, you can't call the operator—my father will hear you.

HELMUT

Not if you cause a distraction.

PETER

You're joking.

HELMUT

You're creative.

PETER

Have you even thought about packing? Supplies? And how're we gonna get into her apartment?

(to audience) He holds up a paper clip.

HELMUT

All we need is this.

PETER

(to audience) He could tell I was faltering. This was three weeks too soon. I wasn't finished my biology paper, I had overdue books out, Arman still owed me money—

HELMUT

Peter, you want this. We want this. I'm telling you, my father will take us in. He'll take care of everything for us once we're over.

PETER

His father had been on the other side when the Wall went up. A door-to-door salesman. Helmut says he went over to fuck a woman one night and found himself stuck. Hope she was worth it. He was the only family he had, as far as I could tell. Though he never told me much about him.

HELMUT

You always want to worry about someone listening in? Having to turn on your record player whenever I come over? Remember: real books, real jobs—and porno! If not for freedom, then do it for the porno!

PETER

(to HELMUT) It's easy for you to say. You gain a father and I lose one.

(to audience) This shut him up for a second. And then he looked right into me.

HELMUT

But think of what you'll gain.

PETER

And this little grin appeared on his face.

You have to understand he was so persuasive. This whole thing was his idea in the first place. The river crossing. Roping Rolf and I into it. And it started just as a joke, really. Something to yak about on our cigarette breaks. But he just kept taking it further and I let him take me along with it.

HELMUT
And don't eat too much. Better to run on an empty stomach.

PETER
(to HELMUT) Less to throw up if they shoot you.

HELMUT
Where does he keep his address book?

PETER
The desk beside the phone in the hallway. Top drawer.

(to audience) I look into the kitchen at my father. Stirring in two exacting spoonfuls of Mocca Fix instant coffee like a chemist. I hate how weak he makes it, like dirty water. I resent him for it the same way I resent him for never reading or listening to music. Just another underwhelming thing about him. What does he know about pleasure? About me? About how much Mother loved him?

Before she left I walked into her room one night. She was sitting on the bed and she looked up. Her eyes were red.

MOTHER
Peter, you should knock.

PETER

She pulled me close to her. We sat in silence for a long while. Watching the street lights flick on. Two bottles of prescription pills on her bedside table. A half glass of water.

MOTHER

You know that I love you. Don't you?

PETER nods.

And so does your father.

PETER

I watched her turn her watch on her wrist. She would do that when she was worried.

MOTHER

If something happens, promise me you'll always look after each other.

PETER

But he looks after us. She smiled.

MOTHER

Sometimes even fathers need someone to look after them. Promise me you'll stay together.

PETER

And I promised.

MOTHER
Your father is not a bad man.

PETER
She left two days later with just the clothes she was wearing. Except her gold watch. She left that on the bedside table, beside the glass of water.

Pause.

She said Father was not a bad man. She never said he was a good man.

FATHER
(calling from the kitchen) Would anyone else like a cup?

PETER
I suddenly realize Helmut's already halfway to the telephone in the hall. I motion for him to stop but he doesn't see me. He reaches the phone and I pretended to choke on a piece of toast to mask the clicking of the receiver. He dials quickly and cuffs the mouthpiece with his hand, just as Father starts back towards the table with the coffee pot and three cups. I jump up to waylay him.

(to FATHER) Let me help!

FATHER
No, no, sit down—

PETER
I make to grab the pot and knock it from his hands—it shatters on the hardwood, a cascade of hot coffee and broken ceramic.

FATHER
Idiot!

PETER
He cuffs me upside the head as we run back into the kitchen, grabbing towels and mopping up the mess, Father picking up each coffee
pot fragment as if it were pieces of a skull. Helmut returns looking
concerned and innocent. My father stands holding the broken pieces
in his hands.

A pause.

HELMUT
Well we'd best be off.

PETER
We move to the door, grabbing our coats. I look back and catch my
father's eye.

FATHER
It's not the fashion, but wear your hard hat. You still have brains in
there somewhere.

PETER
I look at him. He seems small in his housecoat. Holding those shards.

We leave my house running. I take one last look back at my house,
and then let it fall away from me. We weave between men in their hats
and children with satchels, butchers unloading pigs from a truck,
tailors opening their shop windows, a grocer putting out baskets of
apples, past the church where my parents were married and the alley

running behind it where the unshaven choirmaster relieves himself before morning practice. We round a corner and Helmut fumbles in his pocket and removes the address book.

(to HELMUT) I can't believe he didn't notice.

HELMUT
Thanks to your little coffee stunt.

PETER
(to HELMUT) Did you get her number from the operator?

(to audience) He pulls back his sleeve to reveal a phone number scrawled on his wrist. We begin leafing through the addresses looking for the match. Page after page—

HELMUT
Goddamn it, it's not in here.

PETER
We scroll through my father's lists of patients, relatives, friends, acquaintances, classmates, business contacts, living and dead, until we turn the last page and see the number written on the back cover. And below it just the words: Apartment 202, 68 Zimmerstrasse. No name. Just an address. Who is she?

HELMUT
Apartment 202. The second floor. It's jumpable.

PETER
Helmut is almost giddy.

HELMUT

Come on!

PETER

He grabs my hand and we just keep running. His grip so firm, so confident. There's no stopping him now. I glance over at him running beside me. No, I think. There is no stopping him now.

Suddenly, a percussive flash of light/sound. We are back in the present on the Death Strip.

Help! Come on, you bastards! Help me! Please!

(to audience) Frankly, I'm surprised I'm still shouting at this point. What am I expecting? I can tell it unnerves the young guard. I hear him grinding his teeth. His palms are sweaty and his fingers cold. I hear him whispering with his lieutenant:

PETER *whispers.*

"We're supposed to let him bleed out like a pig?"
"We haven't received word yet."
"What if we just sent a medic?"
"He's not our problem."

The sound of a crowd along the Wall, muffled in the distance.

Twenty-six minutes and fifteen seconds: *how could I have been so stupid?* Inside is a burning house, collapsing. But I'm outside of it. Like I am standing on the sidewalk watching the flames licking out of the windows, the roof caving. I can hear the crowd gathering behind me. Their murmurs and jeers. Crowds love a good fire. I was seven years old when our house in Kreuzberg burnt down. There were twenty people watching, but no one did a thing. I guess they thought it was too far gone. I think that was the beginning of the end for my parents. They never loved each other quite the same way in our new house.

I press my back against the Wall. It's a small gift: finding that cool piece of concrete in the shade on a hot day. If I look across towards the East I can see the apartment we jumped from, the window still open, faces in the windows in the building. And the buildings next to it. I look intently into the window. I think of the apartment. Its smells, its secrets. The woman with no name—

A percussive flash of light/sound.

AH.

He breathes through the pain for a long moment.

There's a... shift inside.

He winces, breathes through the pain once more.

Like the shelf has collapsed and the jars have smashed and everything is leaking out—and suddenly I am four, running through our apartment naked, climbing the pantry shelves stocked for winter with mother's pickles and beets, climbing all the way to the top, when suddenly the shelves tip out from the wall, and for a moment I am floating, weightless with the jars, before smashing down. I am lying, crying, naked in blood and brine like I have just been born, when I feel mother's shadow move over me. She picks me up. And holds me.

The sound of PETER crying. The sound of MOTHER comforting him.

Sometimes I imagine she's found her way over and is waiting for me. But then I'll catch glimpses of her. Across parks. In passing cars. Sometimes I'll smell her scent lingering in a store. On a street corner. Once, I even found a strand of her hair on the sidewalk.

You told me to listen close for the answer, but listen to what? There's too much and not enough time, not nearly— Listen closer, she would say, listen closer— And then—

The sound of a camera shutter. And then another.

The sun glints off a zoom lens in the third-floor window of the hotel across the Wall.

The sound of a cigarette smoldering.

The photographer's cigarette smoulders. I can tell by the way his hands sweat as he grips the camera that he is haunted by the task of distilling the despair he feels for the human condition into a single photograph. He takes another picture. And another. And my body, in this picture, will make its way from that negative into the cool chemicals of the dark room to the newspaper's printing press where it'll be pressed into a million little black dots of ink upon three hundred thousand sheets of newsprint and thrown through the city from the sweaty hands of delivery boys as they career on their bikes through the early morning streets still slick with last night's rain. In the morning the city will read all about it with their morning coffee and toast, the moist ring of their cups leaving a bull's eye on my body.

The sound of another camera shutter. And then another. The sounds of a build site.

Four miles away on a build site for a new apartment complex I hear our foreman spit a mouthful of chewed tobacco into a pile of freshly turned concrete—

PETER *imitates his foreman.*

"Those assholes, late a second time this week."

When he hears the news he'll feign disinterest.

"Of course the small one didn't make it over. Always was the other's lapdog."

He'll try, as best as he can, to push us from his mind. But we will linger with him. There's a rumour among the bricklayers that he's haunted by the ghost of a young worker who died on his watch years ago—which would explain his pasty, sleepless look. For everyone knows that ghosts haunt you most when you're asleep.

I think of him, the dead bricklayer and all of the boys, like us, who were hired to begin bricking up the windows of the apartments backing onto the Wall, watching each piece of sky disappear behind mortar. They say it's to keep *them* out, but Helmut says it's to keep us in.

I find myself imagining two hypothetical scenarios for Helmut the moment he landed on the other side of the Wall. In one scenario, he runs eleven straight blocks down Lindenstrasse to the Ministry of Internal Affairs and is wrapped in a reflective blanket and given hot cocoa to drink. I'm not sure why he would need the reflective blanket after running eleven blocks but I imagine the scenario playing out much like that of a plane-crash survivor, so there is the requisite blanket. Maybe they call his father. Maybe his father is already there waiting for him, smiling arm in arm with his one-night stand.

In the second scenario Helmut is standing directly behind the Wall, directly behind me, his hand against the Wall and saying:

HELMUT
I'm right here, Peter. Someone will get you. You're so close. Just hold on.

PETER
I want him to tell me about the American porno. What about the American porno!?

But, in truth, I cannot speak because my mouth is—

He spits blood, surprising himself.

And he cannot hear me for he is probably in a police station six miles away being processed. He always was the fastest in my class. Did he know he could outrun me? If one of us was going to be picked off, he would have known it would be me. He reached the Wall but couldn't make it up so I pushed him. I grabbed his legs and pushed. And I reached up for his hand but it wasn't there. He was already over.

Goddamn him. The way he moved, so lithely, his uncombed hair, his easy laugh, his cockiness. He really was so persuasive. Like just being around him made me... made me do things, not rational things; I didn't think with him, I just felt everything. So deeply. It was like he opened a door and pushed me through it.

Street sounds. PETER *rises. Lights shift.*

We cross Spittelmarkt, out of breath, the address book in Helmut's pocket like a key about to unlock the door to the rest of our lives. Sixty-eight Zimmerstrasse, Apartment 202.

Suddenly there's a commotion up ahead. We watch as a drunkard swears at a dog, swaggering towards it, the emaciated stray too weak to growl but bearing its teeth. The drunkard grabs the stray by the skin of its neck and kicks its belly, once, twice, three times, until we hear its ribs crack. I lock eyes with the grocer across the street and with my eyes I say, "Do something," until I realize his eyes are asking me the same thing. A small crowd forms, no one wanting to walk through the scene. The drunkard smashes the dog's skull with his boot, cursing it, and staggers off, no one saying a word, no one apprehending him. The crowd disperses, surging back along the sidewalk past the shivering dog.

Helmut picks a cigarette up off the street. I notice his hand shaking. He pulls out a small box of matches.

(to HELMUT*)* Where'd you get those?

HELMUT
Top drawer of your old man's desk.

PETER

(to audience) He tosses them to me. I notice the emblem on the box.
Hotel Leibnitz.

HELMUT

A family vacation spot?

PETER

Clients give him gifts.

HELMUT

Matches? From seedy hotels?

PETER

(to audience) I ignore his smirk. We're winded now and slow to
a brisk walk. We cross two more intersections and pass my old
schoolyard, where I spent so much time worrying and learning
about things that never mattered in the end. I watch a group of
kids chasing each other. Two boys throwing a ball against a wall.
Counting down the minutes until the end of recess. Dreading the
bell. The small sinking in your heart when it trills, the realization
time has run out. I feel misplaced suddenly, on the other side of
the fence looking in. As if any second someone will discover I've
snuck out and will come looking for me.

Street sounds—they continue walking.

We walk on, side by side, our arms sometimes brushing together.

(to HELMUT) First thing I want to do is watch all the good movies.
Like *400 Blows*.

HELMUT
Nah, I saw that one. The girl isn't even hot. In the West I'll be getting four hundred blows every week.

PETER
I think we're talking about different movies.

HELMUT
And girls from the West are just hotter, it's a verified fact. There've been studies.

PETER
And our apartment.

HELMUT
Right. Well we'll need to get one together. It's more expensive over there.

PETER
(to audience) Helmut passes me the cigarette. We walk on in silence and I try to imagine our apartment together. The colour of the walls. The grain of the floorboards. Where our beds would be placed.

HELMUT
Look.

PETER
He points across the street. I catch sight of a woman's back behind a curtain in a second-storey window. She reaches back gracefully to unlatch her bra clasp.

HELMUT

I bet she knows we can see her.

PETER

(to audience) You can't die without unlatching a bra clasp, right? Or caressing a thigh? Aren't there rules against that? Cosmic ones? Helmut shakes the box of matches.

HELMUT

So you think your father's bringing ladies to this hotel to fuck them?

PETER

(to HELMUT) Shut up.

HELMUT

It must be hard for him. With your mother gone.

Pause.

Do you know what happened to her?

PETER

She left.

HELMUT

Did she have a reason?

PETER

Of course she had a reason.

HELMUT

Do you think she ran away with someone? Or maybe she found out your father was screwing someone else and she just couldn't take it.

PETER

I think she was brave.

HELMUT

To run away?

PETER

They fell out of love.

HELMUT

So?

PETER

She followed her heart.

HELMUT

Yeah, and broke yours.

PETER

Maybe she had no other choice. Maybe the other option would have been worse. Living loveless. I think that's worse than death, don't you? The possibility of never loving again?

(to audience) Helmut took a long drag on the cigarette and flicked it to the ground.

HELMUT

She ever try to contact you?

PETER

She used to write letters for a few years. Never with her address on them though. First it was every week. Than once a month. And then, after a couple of years, they just stopped.

HELMUT

Maybe she got over. Or the Stasi got her. She was always a little anti-social. Didn't you tell me she kept a cache of banned poetry?

PETER

Yeah, I found them tucked under her bed. I would read them under my blanket with a flashlight, like pornos. Gertrude Stein. She'll knock the bricks outta your head.

(to audience) I'd given Helmut my copy of T.S. Eliot's *The Waste Land* the first week we met. He probably lost it.

HELMUT

Must've been hard for her to keep all those books from your father.

PETER

(to HELMUT) She was a lot better at it than I was.

HELMUT

He found them?

PETER

A couple months back.

HELMUT
Shit.

PETER
He brought me into the kitchen and made me watch as he burned each one in the sink. He didn't know Mother had given them to me. It's like he was burning up the last of her.

HELMUT
How'd he think you got them?

PETER
He thought you gave them to me.

HELMUT
No wonder he burned them.

FATHER
That boy will corrupt you.

PETER
He said it was for my own protection.

FATHER
One day you'll thank me.

PETER
I think in my heart that's when I decided to leave.

HELMUT
Did you tell him that you were the one lending them to me?

PETER

I didn't say anything. I just watched the pages curl back.

(to audience) Helmut dashes across the street, oblivious of traffic. With a confidence that says "Hit me cars, I dare you." I wait for an opening and push through the trudging commuters until I catch up with him.

HELMUT

Do you think he's an informer?

PETER

Who? I look around.

HELMUT

Your father.

PETER

What could the Stasi possibly want to know from him? Who has a cavity in Prenzlauer Berg?

HELMUT

You don't think it's strange, how your old man was always complaining about the Ackermans having company late at night? And where are they this week? Just cleared out.

PETER

People move in and out of the building all the time.

HELMUT

(imitating FATHER*)* "Only anti-social types keep those hours. Just inviting trouble on themselves if you ask me."

PETER

Anyone in the building could've reported them.

HELMUT

The problem with you is you're not watching. You're not listening.

PETER

(to audience) We begin running again, weaving through the congestion, dodging couriers on bikes and shopkeepers dousing sidewalks with buckets. My only thought is of my feet, putting one in front of the other. Keeping pace. Letting everything else fall away.

Finally we turn onto Zimmerstrasse and spot the building. Sixty-eight. Father was right: it's right beside the Wall. But is it close enough?

The sound of the boys walking into the apartment building.

How'll we know if she's still in her apartment or not?

HELMUT

We just buzz 202 and see.

PETER

No, don't—

HELMUT buzzes the apartment.

We wait. After a couple of minutes a man walks in off the street, unlocks the door, and enters. Helmut catches the door with his boot before it shuts.

HELMUT

Come on.

PETER

(whispers) She could be in the shower.

HELMUT

You wish.

PETER

Besides, have you considered whether we can jump two storeys without breaking our legs?

HELMUT

Are you getting cold feet?

PETER

I'm just trying to be realistic.

HELMUT

Come on, I'll race you to the top.

PETER

But— Urgh.

The sound of the boys bounding up a flight of wooden stairs.

We get to the top of the stairs and I see it at the end of the hallway: Apartment 202.

The sound of activity behind closed doors: cooking, babies crying, dogs barking, children getting ready for school, the morning news on the radio. Footsteps down a creaky hallway.

We creep slowly down the hall, families behind closed doors getting ready for the day. For some reason we move like spies trying not to creak the floorboards as if anyone could ever hear us above the noise. When we get to the end of the hall Helmut takes out the paper clip from his pocket, uncurls it, and slides it into the lock and begins to fiddle.

(to HELMUT) I can tell you've done this before.

HELMUT
My old man taught me when I was a kid.

PETER
Only thing mine ever taught me was how to shave. And I still mess that up.

HELMUT
(working the lock) Come on, come on…

PETER
(to audience) Suddenly one of the apartment doors swings open behind us. We freeze. A cat is thrown out into the hall; the door is shut. The cat wanders curiously over to us and nudges Helmut as he fiddles with the lock for two or three minutes before it finally clicks open. We step into Ms. 202's apartment. It's dark. We gently close the door behind us. Suddenly, I hear a man's voice. He's speaking English. A soldier?

HELMUT

(whispers) There's someone in the apartment.

PETER

I hold my breath. My heart beats so loudly I'm sure the man in the next room will hear it.

The sound of a weatherman on the radio listing off temperatures for the weekend.

HELMUT

Wait, it's just—it's the stupid radio.

Gonna be sunny all week.

The sound of the boys entering the kitchen, the fridge humming.

PETER

We enter the small kitchen. I flip a switch. The fluorescent light flickers on. We walk through the kitchen towards her living room. There is a half-eaten piece of toast on a plate. Still a little coffee left in the pot. The weatherman finishes and an American song begins to play in the next room. She's close enough to the Wall to get the signal.

The sound of Patsy Cline's "Crazy" wafting through the space. The sound of the boys walking through the living room.

We walk into the living room and notice an old army radio on the coffee table. It's a chic room: green velvet sofas, beige shag rugs, tall floor lamps. I notice an earmarked copy of Faulkner on the table beside the radio. A coffee-rim stain on the cover. Helmut leafs through her bookshelf.

HELMUT

Not bad. Too many romances of course.

PETER

And then, as if to one-up her, Helmut pulls out *The Waste Land* from his back pocket. The copy I gave him when we first met.

(to HELMUT) You brought a book with you?

HELMUT

I thought it fit the occasion.

PETER

You told me to eat less to make it easier to run and you brought a book?

He flips to the last page. Skims. Looks for the right passage.

HELMUT

"My friend, blood shaking my heart
The awful daring of a moment's surrender
Which an age of prudence can never retract
By this, and this only, we have existed
Which is not to be found in our obituaries"

PETER

(to audience) He pauses for effect.

HELMUT

It means we live and die by our own choices. No one can make them for us. And no one can judge us for them.

PETER

I nod. I'm not entirely sure that's what it means but I let him have his moment. We walk into the woman's bedroom: white bedspread, white curtains. Smells delicate, like a woman.

The sound of drawers being opened.

Helmut opens the dresser drawer and begins digging through underwear. He takes out a brassiere.

HELMUT

Whoa, big tits.

PETER

I begin looking through her dresser as well. Who is Ms. 202? I find a photograph of her in the top drawer. She is plumper than I had imagined: big eyes, girlish cheeks, a jaunty bob cut, and a tight dress that looks too young on her. But attractive in her own way. Imported lipstick. I find a jewellery box. Earrings, pearl necklace, a broach... and a gold watch.

The sound of the watch ticking.

Just like Mother's. It can't be the same. Is it? No. This one's tarnished, and its back looks sanded down. Maybe by some pawnshop owner to cover up a "Made in China" label. Cheap. Definitely second-hand.

Mother's was the real thing: no sanded-down back, no tarnish. A gift from my father the day I was born, on the coldest day since the city began keeping track of such things. Out of the corner of my eye I see Helmut taking off his shirt and putting the brassiere on but I'm too busy looking at the watch—

HELMUT

Hey, Peter, do you think your dad would fancy a fuck?

PETER

Helmut dances around the bedroom in the brassiere. "Stop being such a fairy." He looks at me for a moment and slowly takes it off.

HELMUT

Lighten up.

PETER

I can't. I feel tense. He grabs some long, thin cigarettes from the bedside table, puts two in his mouth, lights them up with Ms. 202's embossed lighter, and hands me one. We smoke on her bed in silence.

HELMUT

What's wrong?

PETER

(to HELMUT) Nothing's wrong.

HELMUT

You're thinking about something.

PETER

I'm thinking I don't want to die before I get laid. Or kissed.

HELMUT

Don't worry about it. Remember, it's a verifiable fact about girls from the West: hotter.

PETER

What's the first thing you're going to do when you get over?

HELMUT

Smoke better cigarettes.

PETER

(to audience) I take a long drag like I see them do in the movies.

PETER coughs.

I even manage to breathe the smoke out through my nose. I know he can tell I'm scared, that I'm running it over and over in my head. He puts his hands on my shoulders and looks into my eyes, deep, like he's searching for something, his face so close that I want to pull away. But I don't.

HELMUT

Don't be afraid. I'll be right beside you.

PETER

I feel his breath on my face. Gentle. Warm. I swallow. I look down and snuff my cigarette in the ashtray. We look at the window from across the room. We both know that's the window. We move to it and assess the distance. It's jumpable.

HELMUT
When you jump, try to roll. It'll break the fall. I've seen them do it in the movies.

PETER
(to HELMUT) Are you crazy? I can't do that. I'll land on my head.

(to audience) We study the guards for a few minutes in silence. The American GIS, the West German soldiers. The GDR soldiers. Where they move. Where they watch. All part of an intricate system.

HELMUT
You see those two towers over there? That's our path: right between those towers. When you hit the ground just don't stop.

PETER
(to HELMUT) What if we can't jump high enough when we get to the Wall?

HELMUT
It's ten feet, we can jump that. Hey—don't stand in the window. We don't want to out ourselves.

PETER
You think we should come back tomorrow?

HELMUT
Why'd we do that?

PETER

I don't know, I just thought—

HELMUT

We ruined her lock; she's going to know someone's been in. We can't come back.

PETER

I'm not ready.

HELMUT

When'll you be more ready than this?

PETER

We're supposed to run in our work boots? They weigh a ton.

HELMUT

Take them off. We'll run in our socks. It'll be easier to climb the Wall that way.

PETER

(to audience) Helmut begins undoing his laces and pulling off his boots.

HELMUT

Look at that; look how close it is, it's *right there.*

Beat.

Don't be afraid. I'm right beside you.

PETER

I undo the laces on my left boot. And then the right. I slowly pull them off. We move towards the window. We look at one another. Helmut smiles. Asshole. We open the window.

Suddenly another rising crescendo of sound: guards shouting, people gathering along the Wall, PETER's heavy breathing, the blood pounding in his head. We've returned to the present at the Wall.

Look. I'm barely here. Almost entirely erased. "Listen closer," she says, "listen closer"—

From where I lay I can hear the young guard with the empty stomach pacing anxiously in the tower. He waits for an order. I hear the sweat run slowly down his neck, under his collar, down his back. I listen to the slow progression of an ingrown hair he irritated while shaving this morning becoming a pimple that will soon join dozens of others adorning his shiny, young face. I imagine him meticulously pinching out each blackhead under the fluorescent hum of the bathroom light each night, taking almost perverse pleasure in it, easing into bed with the satisfaction of a minesweeper.

We hear each minute sound that PETER describes in the following section.

The line erases further—my body, the Wall, the city, a little bird's egg—I hear it crack. It's in a nest on a power line a block from the Wall. It's a sparrow. I don't know the first thing about bird calls but somehow, in this moment, I recognize it. Its little mouth agape. The pink flesh of its throat. The mother inspects and then lifts off. The wind moves through the spaces between her feathers. She flies over the Wall, over the Death Strip, down into the East, into the street, over the heads of people on Leipziger Strasse. She flies over the head of a young woman walking briskly.

I hear the woman's nervous breath moving through her nose, down her windpipe, her lungs expanding, the capillaries contracting and dilating, the blood surging up to her face, making her feel a little flush this morning. She pushes through the doors of a phone booth, pushes a coin into the slot. The coin drops through and rattles with the coins already inside. She begins dialing, each number a different tone, an elaborate system of a thousand voices moving like a current through every telephone wire woven through the city, pulsing with laughter and disappointment and business deals being closed and illicit trysts being made, and I hear this woman's call, travelling at impossible speed amongst them, across neighbourhoods, by windows and birds' nests and past intersections up into a dentist's office on the fourth floor of a new office building on the other side of the city. I hear the quiet squish of the receiver pressed against her ear, her nervous swallow as she waits, the pursing of her lips and the running of her tongue along her teeth to make sure, in her haste, her imported lipstick hasn't smeared there.

The telephone rings on the desk of the receptionist in the dentist's office. She lets the phone ring once, and then again, while eyeing the young boy with freckles and cotton batting in his mouth sitting alone in the waiting room pretending to read a magazine but all the while fantasizing about ejaculating on her breasts. She places the nail file back in the drawer beside the belt her boyfriend forgot on her bedroom floor last night, and as her hand brushes the cold metal buckle she smiles at the thought of him having to discretely hoist his pants up over and over again in front of a roomful of high-powered bankers.

She answers the phone just as my father snaps on his latex gloves in the next room, followed by the whir of his drill, the sucking, gargling, swirling sounds of saliva, all of which are interrupted by the receptionist's entrance, the phone held aloft in her hand—

PETER *imitates the receptionist.*

"It's your sister: she says it's an emergency."

The muffled sounds of Ms. 202 speaking to FATHER *on the telephone.*

As my father grabs the phone I understand that this is a code because my father has no sister. The woman on the phone begins to cry. I hear her chest muscles tightening, the increase of blood flowing through the ventricles of her heart, the breath snagging in her throat, her face flushing redder, the moist, supple sound of her tear ducts secreting, and the clenching of her ass cheeks, which is perhaps unrelated but noteworthy all the same. She tells my father that she was halfway to the bus stop and already late for work when she remembered she'd forgotten to turn the radio off before leaving her apartment and, knowing how it drove her downstairs neighbour Mrs. Düsterbeck crazy, whose bad books she was already in after her toilet backed up and leaked through the ceiling all over the ornate quilt made of the late Mr. Düsterbeck's pyjamas, she ran back to find the door of her apartment unlocked. And not only unlocked but ajar. And not only ajar but forcibly entered with two sets of dirty footprints leading into her apartment, through her kitchen, across her living room, and into her bedroom, where her bedsheets were ruffled, assuming that two vagabonds had had sex in them. She doesn't question how this would be possible in the eleven minutes and forty-two seconds she was out of the apartment. She breathlessly details every drawer in her dresser tampered with, the contents of each drawer, and the placement of the contents as she left them versus the way she found them, taking great pains to detail the manner in which her brassiere was stuffed haphazardly back into a completely different drawer, provoking another flourish of speculations. But most alarming, she tells my father, were two half-smoked cigarettes in the ashtray on her bedside table and her gold watch, usually kept hidden in her jewellery box, laying beside it, as if the buglers or perverts or whoever they were found this prized item, lit two smokes, debated its value, and then decided it wasn't worth the effort to steal.

FATHER

Well these were obviously two-bit thieves who didn't recognize an expensive watch when they saw one. I'll meet you back at your apartment as soon I can. And touch nothing, understand? It's a crime scene now and shouldn't be tampered with.

PETER

And by now I realize, of course, that this woman in the phone booth is Ms. 202, and I realize that it's rather likely my father's been sticking more than his drill in her mouth, and I see in that moment three years of illicit hotel-room trysts and unconventional lovemaking involving plastic toys imported from the USSR.

The sound of the watch ticking.

I hear the steady and persistent sound of the gold watch ticking on her bedside table. My mother's watch, for there was only ever one. As I lay listening to it tick beside the bed, in the apartment, behind the security fence, across the Death Strip, I imagine my father taking my mother's watch, the one he gave her the day I was born on the coldest day since the city began keeping track of such things, and bringing it into the jewellers to have the back lightly sanded, not to hide a "Made in China" label or a second-hand imperfection, but to erase the name he had had engraved there eighteen years earlier.

And from across the city I hear the choir leader at the church where my parents were married zip up his fly, which had been down since his morning visit to the alley. He scratches his pubic hair once, twice, clears his throat, turns to the boys in their velvet robes, and raises his hands.

The sound of "Rejoice, O Virgin" from Rachmaninov's Vespers can be heard, starting low, and then building. A sustained, ecstatic moment.

These voices. I will never know the bodies these voices belong to. But then, maybe they don't belong to bodies. To any one body. Maybe a voice will go through many bodies in its life.

The hymn begins to merge with crowd jeers, distant and muffled.

The crowd is growing louder, but they're far from me now. Like a storm rolling off from a shore, no longer a concern, just as neither the cold of the concrete nor the burning of my stomach is a concern.

The sound of FATHER *climbing into a taxicab.*

I hear my father climb into the taxicab.

FATHER
Sixty-eight Zimmerstrasse.

The muffled sounds of the cab driver speaking with FATHER.

PETER

The driver smiles and says he thinks he knows the one and then apologizes for the state of his dented bumper, launching into a story of how a car rear-ended him that morning and how the young men didn't even stop, didn't even apologize, and as he drives the story slowly segues into a eulogy for the city at large, the Berlin the driver once knew full of courteous neighbours, and that, as an old man, he drives through the streets he once knew like his daughter's face and doesn't even recognize his own home, as if the Wall cut us off not only from our families but from our reason, our human faculties for decency and judgment. I hear the metre in the cab ticking off the price with every block, hear it pulling up in front of 68, the driver complaining about what a wretched location for an apartment, so close to the Wall, and that he hears they'll begin tearing buildings like this down or bricking them up, being such a liability and all, as my father's hand searches his pockets for change, mumbling—

FATHER

I suggest you brick up your mouth.

PETER

I hear Father stride into the lobby, no longer shuffling but for once lifting his feet, his shoes echoing on the art-nouveau tiling, up the flight of wooden stairs, and he's breathless now as he jogs down the hall with its barking dogs and cooking smells, and knocking on the door of apartment 202 once, twice, and then turning the knob, knocking again as he opens the door.

FATHER
Hello?

PETER
He follows our dirty footprints slowly through the empty kitchen, past the hum of the fridge and the half-eaten toast and the coffee still in the coffee pot. Slowly through the empty living room.

FATHER
Hello?!

PETER
Past the green velvet sofas and the beige shag carpet and the ear-marked copy of Faulkner and the radio softly playing American standards and into the bedroom with its ruffled white bedspread and haphazardly opened drawers and the two half-smoked cigarettes beside the gold watch. The gold watch he brought into a jewellers the week his wife walked out the front door, never to return, and had her name sanded off because he is only human goddamn it and why shouldn't he be allowed to feel new love coursing through his veins again? And he turns to the window, the bedroom window, where a woman stands silhouetted against the midday sun, beside two pairs of work boots sitting side by side—the woman whose distress made him cancel an appointment for the first time since his son was born, and not only one appointment but three! He watches her in the window watching something by the Wall.

FATHER
I came as fast as I could.

PETER

She does not turn. Is she crying? No, her shoulders aren't moving. What is she looking at, he wonders.

FATHER

Did they escape through the window?

PETER

He moves towards her. Presses his stomach against her back, wrapping his arm around her chest. He whispers in her ear that it'll be okay. He smells her. He feels the beat of her heart, her shallow breath, and tries to slow it with the steady, insistent rise and fall of his own chest on her back. And then he follows her gaze with his eyes. He sees the two sets of footprints first. Their impact just on the other side of the fence: one with handprints beside the feet to brace his fall, the other with a cleaner landing, just the imprint of two feet. And from the point of impact two frenzied routes across the Death Strip, weaving at one point apart and then growing closer together, one jumping the first set of barbed wire, the other choosing to shimmy through it, and then both paths converging on almost the same point on the Wall... And then a body.

FATHER

Oh my god.

PETER

The body of a boy, five feet, seven inches, one hundred and forty pounds—maybe a hundred and forty-two after a big meal—brown hair, brown eyes, curled on his side like a kicked dog, like he was trying to hold himself together. I feel my father's growing recognition. His growing comprehension. He is shouting but I do not hear his words, not over the ticking of the gold watch on the bedside table, the obscene ticking which I know, in this moment, my father hears too, but now for the first time through my ears, through my illicit discovery of it in this apartment. It's the sound of me knowing his secret and him knowing I know his secret.

PETER *turns and finds his* FATHER's *eyes with his eyes.*

I see him.

And he sees me.

Look at us. Alone and afraid. Him in the window, me on the rocks. Two gutted fish.

I look into his eyes. Blue. Almost grey. I have his eyes. I never noticed before.

With my eyes I ask him, "Do you love her?"

FATHER
Does it matter? Don't we all need the warmth of a body? To help us through the cold of our lives.

PETER
I hope it was worth it.

FATHER
And was it worth it for you? For a bricklayer?

PETER

You think I jumped for a—?

Silence.

A boy on a red bike. A race up a flight of stairs, a jimmied lock, a smile daring me to jump, to just jump into our lives together.

I lifted him over and waited. I waited for his hand. I waited.

Pause.

It was so stupid.

Pause.

But yes. I would do it again. Because what if I hadn't? What if I'd never known? Isn't that worse?

The sound of a sustained tone begins to build in the background.

And in this moment I understand that across this city and farther, maybe everywhere, people are destroying themselves for love. I see myself by the Wall and Ms. 202 and my father in the window and a phone left hanging off the hook in a phone booth and a man giving a presentation without a belt and a nest full of sparrows crying for their mother on a telephone pole and a taxi driver mourning the death of his city and a lonely man with a camera on the third floor of a hotel and an unshaven choirmaster leading voices without bodies and a young guard with his empty stomach and sore tongue who just wants to go home to a few pieces of warm toast. I hear every brick of a new apartment complex four miles away being laid, every brick in its proper place, building apartments for young couples to live in and dream in and grow disenchanted and die in. All the bricklayers going about their work, all destined to haunt someone with their death someday, all the while oblivious to the persistent longing that pervades every detail of their waking lives.

The sound of a passenger plane flying overhead.

I hear two hundred and thirty-six passengers in a flight from Stuttgart a half vertical mile overhead flying away from or towards love.

The sound of the airplane's interior: passengers talking quietly amongst themselves.

I hear the voices of the people on the plane. Talking about the trip ahead, the weather, a bit of gossip. Someone laughs. Someone is reading a book. There is a dog in a cage in the cargo hold who is afraid and alone.

The pages of a book being turned. A dog barking. The sound of knitting.

A grandmother knits a red sweater for her grandson, who will need it sooner than she realizes because—

The sound of wind, low and distant.

—farther still, I hear a massive cold front moving in, the water condensing in the clouds and the water droplets slowly crystallizing into a perfect, gentle snowfall. Because even the earth tries to outdo itself for us from time to time. Even though we seldom take notice.

The sound of a watch ticking.

Fifty-eight minutes and twelve seconds. The gold watch on the bedside table is ticking.

The ants burrow deep, the crickets scream.

"These fragments I have shored against my ruins."

A pair of boots.

I see boots walking towards me.

The murmur of the guards, the static blips of their walkie-talkies.

Helmut. You came back.

His shadow moves over me.

I feel him lift me. He has the face of the young guard. He is crying.

He carries me in his arms.

He carries me over.

He carries me—

The sound of the watch ticking stops just as the time on the digital readout runs out: 00:00.

Blackout.

End of play.

Playwright's Acknowledgements

A very special thank you to Annie Gibson, Blake Sproule, and the Playwrights Canada Press team for believing in this collection. To Julian Montague for his beautiful cover. To Rae Powell for her steadfast support over the years as Suburban Beast's co-founder and production manager. To Erin Brubacher for her exacting editorial eye. To my loving family for being a continual source of inspiration and encouragement. And, most of all, to my love William Ellis, for being there every step of the way.

For *Get Yourself Home Skyler James*: Thank you to David S. Craig, Natasha Greenblatt, Alisa Palmer, Krista MacIsaac, Lucinda Zak, Patterson Fardell, Bryde MacLean, the Canadian Stage Company, Toronto's Triangle Program, and the Toronto District School Board's Equity and Human Sexuality Departments. My sincerest gratitude to Skyler James for her candour and courage. This play is for you, Skyler.

For *rihannaboi95*: Thank you to Owais Lightwala, Zack Russell, Naomi Skwarna, Jon Davies, Andrew Kushnir, Antonio Cayonne, Catherine Murray, Project: Humanity, Youth Without Shelter, Covenant House, Roseneath Theatre, and Carousel Players.

For *Peter Fechter: 59 Minutes*: Thank you to Christian Barry, Tommie Olajide, Richard Feren, Rae Powell, Tye Hunt Fitzgerald, Ben Carson, the WYE, Brendan Healy, Erika Hennebury, Buddies in Bad Times Theatre, the Toronto Arts Council, the Ontario Arts Council, the Canada Council for the Arts, Vicki Stroich, Colleen Wagner, the Banff Centre for the Arts Playwrights Colony, and Volcano Theatre.

Jordan Tannahill is a playwright, director, and filmmaker. Through his Dora Award–winning company Suburban Beast, Jordan creates performances exploring the lives of diverse Torontonians, many of whom collaboratively create and perform in the work. His plays include *Concord Floral, Post Eden, Honesty, Feral Child, Bravislovia,* and *The Art of Catching Pigeons by Torchlight.* Jordan's play *Late Company* won the 2013 Herman Voaden Playwriting Competition, the Enbridge playRites Award, and the Audience Choice and Best Production Awards for its production at the 2013 SummerWorks Festival. Jordan was the 2011 recipient of the Inside Out Film Festival's Emerging Canadian Artist Award, the 2011 Ken McDougall Award for Emerging Directors, and was shortlisted for the 2012 Ingmar Bergman Prize. His films have screened across Canada and internationally. He runs a store-front theatre called Videofag in Toronto's Kensington Market with his partner William Christopher Ellis.

Printed and bound in Canada by General Printers, Oshawa.

Cover design & illustration by Julian Montague
Book design by Blake Sproule

PLAYWRIGHTS
CANADA PRESS
202-269 Richmond St. W.
Toronto, ON
M5V 1X1

416.703.0013
info@playwrightscanada.com
www.playwrightscanada.com

MIX
Paper from
responsible sources
FSC® C023656
www.fsc.org